Creative Paper Dollmaking

Rhonda Rainey

Sterling Publishing Co., Inc. New York
A Sterling / Chapelle Book

Chapelle:
Owner: Jo Packham
Editor: Cathy Sexton
Art Director: Karla Haberstich
Staff: Areta Bingham, Kass Burchett,
Ray Cornia, Marilyn Goff, Holly
Hollingsworth, Susan Jorgensen,
Emily Kirk, Barbara Milburn, Karmen
Quinney, Caroll Shreeve, Cindy Stoeckl,
Kim Taylor, Sara Toliver, Desirée Wybrow

Photography: Kevin Dilley for Hazen Imaging, Inc.

Photo Stylist: Jill Dahlberg

If you have any questions or comments or would like
information on specialty products featured in this book,
please contact:
Chapelle, Ltd., Inc.
P.O. Box 9252, Ogden, UT 84409
(801) 621-2777 • (801) 621-2788 Fax
e-mail: chapelle@chapelle ltd.com
web site: www.chapelleltd.com

Library of Congress Cataloging-in-Publication Data Available

Rainey, Rhonda.
   Creative paper dollmaking / Rhonda Rainey.
   p. cm.
   "A Sterling/Chapelle book."
   Includes index.
   ISBN 0-8069-9187-9
   1. Paper doll making. I. Title.

   TT175 .R32 2002
   745.592'21--dc21

                         2002030857

10 9 8 7 6 5 4 3 2 1

Published by Sterling Publishing Co., Inc.
387 Park Avenue South, New York, NY 10016
© 2003 by Rhonda Rainey
Distributed in Canada by Sterling Publishing
c/o Canadian Manda Group, One Atlantic Avenue, Suite 105
Toronto, Ontario, Canada M6K 3E7
Distributed in Great Britain by Chrysalis Books
64 Brewery Road, London N7 9NT, England
Distributed in Australia by Capricorn Link (Australia) Pty. Ltd.
P.O. Box 704, Windsor, NSW 2756, Australia
Printed and Bound in China
All Rights Reserved

Sterling ISBN 0-8069-9187-9

tribal dancer journal

table of contents

P. 16

P. 49

P. 10

P. 63

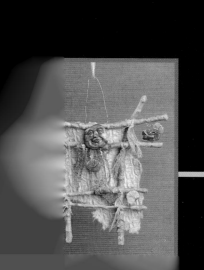

P. 74

P. 90

looking back . . .

Paper dolls, throughout the ages, have given pleasure and have captivated the imaginations of those who have played with, collected, studied, and designed them. Paper, as we know it today, was first made in China approximately 105 A.D. Although it is impossible to give an exact date, it is generally acknowledged that small paper figures were used in Chinese religious ceremonies about this same time.

Several hundred years later, after the Japanese learned the art and craft of papermaking, the use of doll-like figures cut or folded from paper became a part of ancient purification ceremonies in their culture. A small paper figure was rubbed on the body of the person wishing to be cleansed of his sins. It was then flung into a river or the ocean and washed away.

In the 1200s, Marco Polo wrote in his journals about paper figures, recognizable as male and female forms, being destroyed, along with the body, as part of Chinese funeral rites.

Many years passed before the papermaker's art made its way to Europe and paper mills were established in Spain, Italy, and France. Paper, although limited in supply, became available to those who could afford it. By the mid 1700s, the cost of paper and printing and the idea of leisure time came together in such a way that toys, and time to enjoy them, were allowed for children and adults. Leisure time or playtime was a novel idea to the people of the 18th century.

The first paper dolls used as amusement were thought to have come from the French court of Louis XV. String puppets, called pantins, and fashion dolls were in high vogue.

Pantins, paper jumping jacks, were an old German toy with a new name when the craze swept Paris in the mid 1700s.

They were engraved on thin paper and sold to be colored, cut, and assembled at home. Others were completed by the printer and some pieces were finished by famous painters of the time. After color was added to the engraved images, they were pasted onto cardboard, cut out, then threaded at the joints. All parts of the body were separate and were attached by strings at the back of the figure. They could then be made to dance or get into contorted positions by pulling on a master thread. Most pantins measured 4" to 28" in height. The characters were varied. Favorite subjects included clowns such as Colombine and Harlequin, milkmaids, soldiers, shepherds, shepherdesses, and of course, notable personalities and court figures in disguise (they were not always represented in the best light!) All articulated paper dolls owe their beginnings to the French pantin.

Small French dolls called "couriers of fashion" preceded the pantin by more than 100 years. By the mid 1500s three-dimensional figures were being dressed in the finest styles of the French court and exported to the courts and capitals of Europe. These dolls were costly and generally not intended as play things. Old records note that they were created from a kind of paper and paste which was pressed into hollow molds, then air-dried and hardened. During the 1700s, these fashion dolls became so popular that their export was regulated by a bureau or registry. This practice continued into the late 19th century. It was not long before the Pandoras, or Milliner's Models as they were affectionately called, became available to the general public. These little messengers carried the most current styles in dressmaking and hairdressing to the civilized world.

In the late 1700s, hand-colored fashion plates became a popular way to introduce new fashions. These plates had several advantages over the three-dimensional dolls—among them, ease of distribution and the number of pieces that could be sent out.

It is interesting to note that fashion and domestic magazines made their appearance in England and on the continent at about this same time. Cutout paper sheets showing a character standing in profile, dressed in a short shift, and accompanied by a selection of dresses that could be cut out, then placed flat over the figure, made their debut in these early publications. Two hundred years later, in a new millennium, cutout dolls are still published in popular magazines.

Today, dimensional dolls are more popular than ever. Some are so sophisticated that they surpass the idea of "doll" and become sculpture. Globally, collectors are seeking the new and unusual as well as the traditional in doll art. Many of the materials used to create dolls of the past are still in use today; however, new paper-based products have expanded the term "paper doll." These new materials, as well as the availability of lovely and unusual papers from around the world have changed the face of doll making and paper artistry. Today's doll artists are pushing the boundaries of what paper dolls are and can be.

The projects in this book include a variety of styles and techniques. Many can be used interchangeably. A number of the simpler projects can be added to or used as a "springboard" for more complex ideas. As with any creative endeavor—imagination knows no bounds! I hope you find, as I did, some surprises, a sense of discovery, and joy in the journey.

Design tip:

Paper-twist ribbon can be substituted for the skirt material instead of using florist's foil. Simply crimp the ribbon and gather it along the top edge to fit the waistline of the cut-out angel or figure you are using.

simply victorian

List of supplies:

- Acrylic paint, metallic gold
- Card stock, heavy
- Craft glue
- Embellishments
- Embroidery floss
- Florist's foils: assorted colors
- Greeting cards or reproduction Victorian art images
- Paint applicator, ultrafine tip
- Scissors, sharp

Instructions:

1. Using scissors, cut out angels (from heads to waists) and flowers from greeting cards or reproduction Victorian art images.

2. Using a paint applicator, outline all edges with metallic gold paint. Allow to dry.

Hint: This is easiest if all pieces are laid out separately on a piece of scrap paper.

3. To make each skirt, cut a piece of florist's foil to the desired length and two times the desired width. Make a $^1/_4$" fold along hemline. Working from left to right, make $^1/_4$" knife pleats as shown in Diagram A at right until skirt is the desired width. Fan-out by gently pushing pleats at waistline closer together and spreading pleats at hemline farther apart.

Diagram A

4. Attach skirts to angels at waistlines with craft glue. Add flowers (from largest to smallest). Let dry.

5. To finish the backs, glue angels onto card stock. Let dry.

Hint: Place under a heavy book to help prevent warping.

6. Cut angels from card stock and embellish as desired.

7. To make the hangers, double a length of embroidery floss and knot the ends together to make a loop for hanging. Glue onto top center of each ornament.

striking a pose

rose doll tassel

List of supplies:

- Acrylic paints:
  dark brown, flesh,
  pale blue-green,
  yellow-green,
  dark rose, rose,
  white pearl, yellow

- Acrylic varnish spray,
  satin finish

- Brass charm,
  celestial sun face

- Card stock, heavy

- Cloth, lint-free

- Coffee filters, white,
  8"-round

- Cornstarch

- Craft glue

- Creative Paperclay®
  modeling compound,
  white, 3 oz.

- Découpage medium,
  satin finish

- Disposable cups

- Embroidery flosses,
  6-strand:
  light green, 10 yards;
  light yellow, 5 yards

- Garlic press

(Continued on page 13)

Instructions:

1. Using a paintbrush, apply two coats of découpage medium to mug peg. Let dry between each coat.

2. Using a dry paintbrush, dust the inside of the brass charm with cornstarch.

3. Pinch off one pea-sized piece of modeling compound, roll into a ball, and press into brass charm.

Hint: If clay does not easily release, press another pea-sized ball of modeling compound onto back of clay in mold to act as a handle. Lift and release clay from mold and gently separate the "face" from the clay handle. Discard handle.

4. Apply a thin layer of découpage medium to one side of the rounded part of mug peg. Attach molded face, blending edges with additional découpage medium. Let dry.

5. Make several additional pea-sized balls of modeling compound. To make curls, squeeze each ball of modeling compound through a garlic press. Roll coils into curls and attach as in Step 4 above.

6. To make the arms, roll modeling compound into $1/2$" coils. Shape arms as desired and attach as in Step 4 above. Let dry for 24 hours.

7. Apply two coats of découpage medium to all areas. Let dry between each coat.

8. Using the paintbrush, paint face, neck, and shoulders with flesh. Paint body and arms with yellow-green, blending edges at shoulders. Paint gloves with pale blue-green. Let dry.

9. To antique the face, dip tip of paintbrush into dark brown, then into glazing medium. Brush over face, working into recessed areas around eyes, nose, and mouth. Wipe with a dry lint-free cloth to remove excess. Let dry.

Hint: If antique finish looks too dark, add a drop of glazing medium and work into recessed areas before paint dries.

10. Paint lips with dark rose, cheeks with rose, eyelids with green, and hair with white pearl and yellow 1:1. Let dry.

11. Spray with two light coats of acrylic varnish. Let dry between each coat.

(Continued from page 12)

- Glazing medium, clear
- Hand-sewing needle
- Jump ring, $1/8$"
- Metallic thread
- Organza ribbon, $3/4$"-wide, pink, 1 yard
- Paintbrush, #6 round
- Satin roses, pink (2)
- Scissors, sharp
- Screw eyes, 5mm (2)
- Thread
- Wooden ball-top mug peg, $2 1/2$"
- Wooden pencil, round, unsharpened

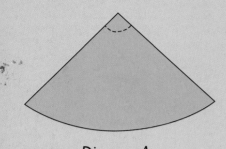

Diagram A

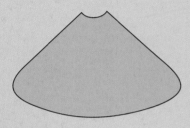

Diagram B

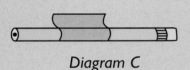

Diagram C

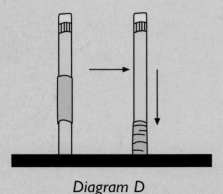

Diagram D

12. Fold three coffee filters into quarters and crease. Using scissors, cut a semicircle shape from the tip as shown in Diagram A at left. To make the petals, cut along creases (from the bottoms to the tops). Trim the bottom corners, rounding out each of the petals as shown in Diagram B at left.

13. Using the Calyx Leaf Pattern on page 15, cut out six leaves from coffee filters.

14. Mix two drops of rose paint and two teaspoons of water in a disposable cup. Using the paintbrush, paint petals. Let dry.

Hint: For more intense color, mix and add more paint as desired.

15. Mix one drop of pale blue-green paint, one drop of yellow paint, and two teaspoons of water in a disposable cup. Paint leaves. Let dry.

16. To crimp the petals, lightly roll each petal around an unsharpened pencil as shown in Diagram C at left. Hold the unsharpened end of the pencil perpendicular to the table and firmly push the petal downward as shown in Diagram D at left. Remove and smooth. Repeat with each petal, working from top to bottom and from side to side. Roll and crimp edges and shape with fingers.

17. To crimp the leaves, repeat Step 16 above.

18. Using a hand-sewing needle and a doubled length of thread, make small running stitches at the top of each petal. Stitch all four petals onto thread, tightly gathering and adjusting gathers to fit around doll's hips. Tie off. Attach first layer of skirt into place with craft glue. Repeat stitching and gathering for remaining two sets of petals. Offset each layer as they are attached. Recurl petal tips with a pencil.

19. Using five of the leaves, repeat Step 18 above for leaves around waistline.

20. To make the tassel, neatly wind light green embroidery floss and light yellow embroidery floss around a 4"-square of card stock. Using embroidery floss, tightly tie off at top. Remove from card stock and cut bottom. To form the tassel head, wind the top $^3/_8$" of tassel with embroidery floss. Attach a jump ring at top of tassel. Attach a screw eye to the jump ring, then screw into bottom of mug peg.

21. Tightly wrap organza ribbon around waistline twice and tie a bow at back. Glue satin roses under bow.

22. Attach a screw eye to top of head making certain it is screwed into the wood and not just into the modeling compound hair.

23. To make the hat, glue remaining leaf to head covering the screw eye. Make a small organza ribbon bow and glue to side of hat.

24. To make the hanger, slip a length of metallic thread through the screw eye at top of tassel and knot the ends together to make a loop for hanging.

25. Holding the tassel in your hand, spray with two light coats of acrylic varnish. Let dry between each coat.

Design tip:

The process of crimping creates a paper which has much the same feel as old-fashioned crepe paper. It will give a crisp piece of paper a fabric-like texture and appearance.

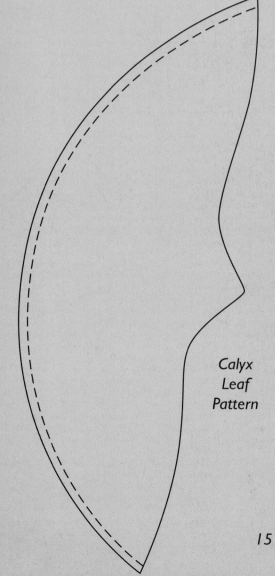

Calyx
Leaf
Pattern

15

pinecone santa

a festive fellow

Instructions:

1. To make the papier-mâché pulp, soak 15 feet of 2-ply toilet paper in a dishpan filled with cool water for approximately 10 minutes.

2. Using a wire whisk, beat the toilet paper and water mixture until paper is "soupy."

Hint: It may be necessary to add more water as the pulp must be extremely wet.

3. Pour the pulp through a sieve, gently shaking to remove as much water as possible, but do not press the water out of the pulp.

4. Place drained pulp in a mixing bowl. Add $1/4$ teaspoon cellulose powder per three cups of pulp. Using a table fork, mix well and let sit for approximately 10 minutes. Mix with hands until mixture is the consistency of mashed potatoes and feels slightly sticky.

Hint: If the mixture is too wet, some of the moisture can be blotted off with a pad of paper towels.

5. Using scissors, cut an $8^{1}/_{2}$" x 11" sheet of card stock into four $4^{1}/_{4}$" x $5^{1}/_{2}$" pieces.

6. To make the "bones" for the arms and legs, roll each piece of card stock, one at a time along the $4^{1}/_{4}$" side, around a pencil. Secure the edges with masking tape and remove the "tubes" from the pencil.

7. Place a paper towel flat on a rigid surface. Place a walnut-sized piece of papier-mâché on the paper towel and flatten until it is approximately $1/4$" thick. Remove papier-mâché from the paper towel and wrap around one of the tubes. Repeat until all four tubes are covered with papier-mâché. Air-dry for 24 hours or oven-dry at 200° for one hour.

8. To make the head, cover a plastic egg with a $1/4$"-thick layer of papier-mâché. Smooth with fingers, smoothing and blending as necessary. Let dry.

List of supplies:

- Acrylic paints: black, brown, flesh, pink, white

- Acrylic varnish spray, satin finish

- Bamboo skewer

- Buttons with metal shanks (2)

- Card stock, tan, $8^{1}/_{2}$" x 11" sheets (6)

- Cellulose powder

- Corsage pin

- Craft glue

- Creative Paperclay® modeling compound, white, 6 oz.

- Découpage medium, satin finish

(Continued on page 18)

(Continued from page 17)

- Doll needle, 4"
- Floral wire, 20-gauge
- Gesso, white
- Hair, cotton thread
- Hand-sewing needle
- Masking tape
- Measuring cups
- Measuring spoons
- Mixing bowl, large
- Needle-nosed pliers
- Paintbrush, #6 round
- Paper punch, 1" leaf
- Paper towels
- Plastic bottle, 20 oz.
- Plastic dishpan, 12-quart
- Plastic egg, $2^3/4$" tall
- Ribbon or braid
- Scissors, sharp
- Sieve, fine
- Table fork
- Thread
- Toilet paper, 2-ply, 1 roll
- Toothbrush, stiff-bristle
- Toothpick, round
- Velvet, dark green
- Wire whisk
- Wooden pencil, round
- Wrapping tissue, patterned

18

9. Form mittens and boots from the papier-mâché. Let dry.

Hint: Make mittens a bit smaller at top so they will fit sleeve area when joined.

10. To make the body, cover a plastic bottle, including the bottom, with a $1/4$"-thick layer of papier-mâché. Smooth with fingers, smoothing and blending as necessary. Let dry.

Hint: Make certain to remove the lid from the plastic bottle before covering it.

11. Continue covering arms and legs with $1/4$" layers of papier-mâché until they measure approximately 2" in diameter. Let dry between each layer.

12. Roll four 1"-diameter "balls" from papier-mâché. To make the shoulders, attach one ball to one end of each arm. Slightly flatten shoulders. Using a toothpick, make a hole through the shoulder of each arm while wet. Attach one ball to the top of each leg. Make a hole through the tops of each leg, from top to bottom, while wet. Allow to dry.

13. Using a stiff-bristle toothbrush and brown paint thinned to a watery consistency, spatter five sheets of card stock. Let dry.

Hint: Make certain to protect surrounding areas from stray paint spatters. A cardboard box works well as a spatter box.

14. Using a leaf-shaped paper punch, punch out numerous leaves from spattered card stock.

15. Pinch off pea-sized pieces of modeling compound and cover entire surfaces of head, mittens, and boots to create a smooth finish. Add facial details. Let dry.

Hint: Dampening your fingers with water will make the smoothing process easier.

16. Using a paintbrush, apply gesso to areas at shoulders, wrists, and bottoms of legs. Apply gesso to body. Let dry.

17. Paint face with flesh, eyes with black, eyebrows with white, and cheeks and lips with pink. Paint boots with black. Let dry.

18. Beginning at cuff edge of each sleeve, attach leaf punchouts in an overlapping "scale" pattern around arms with craft glue. Apply glue to top area of leaves only. The first rows should extend past the edge approximately $1/4$"–$1/2$". Continue to within 1" of top of arms.

Hint: The tops of each mitten will fit under the edge when the mittens are attached.

19. Repeat Step 18 above for both legs, gluing leaf punchouts all the way to the top of the legs.

Hint: Do not cover the hole at the top of each leg.

20. Randomly tear small pieces from wrapping tissue. Using the paintbrush, apply wrapping tissue pieces to shoulders, mittens, and body with découpage medium. Let dry.

21. Embellish Santa's suit with buttons and a belt (made from ribbon or braid).

Design tips:

A purchased velvet bag can be filled with miniature toys and wrapped candies, then placed at Santa's side for display.

Santa can be made to sit instead of to stand by stretching the wires when attaching the legs during Step 22 on page 20.

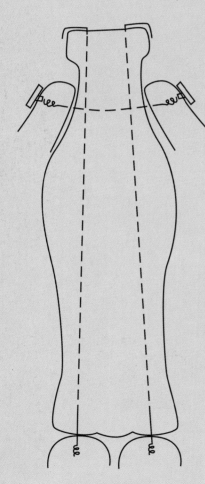

Diagram A

22. Determine leg placement at bottom of body. Using a doll needle, make one hole through the body to accommodate each leg. Using needle-nosed pliers, wind and knot one end of each 18" length from floral wire. To attach legs to body, thread one length of wire up through the bone in each leg (the knot will secure the wire), out through the hole at the top of each leg, and into the appropriate hole in the bottom of the body. Push wire out through the opening at the neck as shown in Diagram A at left. Using needle-nosed pliers, snugly pull wire up and over top rim of bottle neck as shown. Crimp wire tightly to secure and trim if necessary.

23. Determine arm placement at sides of body. Using the doll needle, make one hole through the body to accommodate each arm. Thread one 18" length of floral wire through the shank of one button. Tightly pull and twist to secure. Thread the wire through the arm, then through the first hole in the side of the body, continuing through the body, exiting at the hole on the other side of the body, through the other arm, and finally through the shank of the remaining button as shown in Diagram A. Using needle-nosed pliers, tightly pull and twist to secure. Clip wire end and tuck under button.

24. Attach head to neck with modeling compound. Let dry.

25. Attach mittens to arms and boots to legs with craft glue. Make certain to position mittens and boots under the first layers of leaf punchouts. Let dry.

26. Spray with three light coats of acrylic varnish. Let dry between each coat.

27. Glue beard in place and then glue hair in place.

28. To make the hat, cut one 6$\frac{1}{2}$"-diameter circle from velvet. Hand-sew a $\frac{1}{8}$" rolled hem with small running stitches. Pull to gather, making opening to fit around Santa's head. Tie off. Shape hat and embellish as desired.

29. Using needle-nosed pliers, secure hat by pushing a corsage pin firmly into head.

30. To "curl" the tips of the leaf punchouts (pinecone petals), roll tips around a bamboo skewer.

31. Cover beard and hair, then spray with two light coats of acrylic varnish. Let dry between each coat.

vintage paper doll frame

the best of times

List of supplies:

- Acrylic paints: ivory, soft yellow
- Acrylic varnish, satin finish
- Color photocopy of original artwork of paper dolls, clothing, and accessories
- Découpage medium, satin finish
- Gesso, white
- Glazing medium, clear
- Paintbrush, ¹/₂" flat
- Paper towels
- Rubbing alcohol
- Scissors, sharp
- Wooden frame

Design tip:

For an aged appearance, crackling medium can be used on the frame after it has been painted. Add your selected cutouts and embellish your frame as desired.

Instructions:

1. Using a paper towel, wipe surface of frame with rubbing alcohol.

2. Using a paintbrush, apply a light coat of acrylic varnish to frame. Allow to dry.

3. Apply two coats of gesso to frame. Let dry between each coat.

4. Paint frame with ivory. Without rinsing paintbrush, pick up a small amount of glazing medium and soft yellow paint. Apply with soft, feathery strokes in a random pattern. Let dry.

Hint: This gives an aged appearance rather than one with contrast.

5. Apply a coat of découpage medium to frame. Let dry.

6. Using scissors, cut the paper doll, clothing, and accessories from a color photocopy made from original artwork.

Hint: Using a color photocopy of artwork is ideal for projects such as this. It allows the original to be preserved. In addition, the size can be adjusted to accommodate the scale and shape of the frame. Last, all of the cutouts will be of uniform thickness.

7. Determine the cutout placement on frame. Apply découpage medium to frame and adhere cutouts.

8. Apply a light coat of découpage medium to cutouts, beginning at centers of individual images and working toward outsides. Apply two additional light coats of découpage medium to frame. Let dry between each coat.

The artwork on page 23 may be color-copied and used to decorate your frame. Stickers, cutouts, and brass charms which repeat the themes can be added for additional embellishment.

List of supplies:

- Acrylic paints: black, flesh, dark pink
- Acrylic varnish, satin finish
- Buttons: 2-hole $1/4$" (2); 4-hole $1/4$" (2)
- Cornstarch
- Cotton fabric, $1/8$ yard
- Craft knife, sharp
- Creative Paperclay® modeling compound, white, 6 oz.
- Decorative buckle, $1/2$"
- Découpage medium, satin finish
- Dental floss
- Doll needle, 4"
- Grosgrain ribbon, $1/2$"-wide
- Hand-sewing needle
- Hook-and-eye fastener
- Paintbrushes: #6 round, #00 round
- Plastic egg, $2 1/2$" tall
- Push molds: face, hands, feet
- Rolling pin
- Sandpaper, extra-fine
- Scissors, sharp
- Thread
- Toothpick
- Waxed paper

off the wall

humpty dumples

Instructions:

1. Using a #6 round paintbrush, apply two light coats of acrylic varnish to plastic egg. Let dry between each coat.

2. Pinch off one 1"-sized piece of modeling compound and add one or two drops of water. Knead into a soft dough-like consistency.

3. Place modeling compound on a sheet of waxed paper. Using a rolling pin, roll to $1/8$" thickness. Remove modeling compound from the waxed paper and wrap around the plastic egg. Repeat until plastic egg is completely covered with modeling compound. Let dry.

4. Using a dry paintbrush, dust inside of push molds with cornstarch.

5. Pinch off pea-sized pieces of modeling compound, roll into a ball, and press into face push mold. Release mold. Let set for approximately 30 minutes.

6. Using a craft knife, carefully trim excess modeling compound from back of molded face until it is approximately $1/2$" thick.

7. Determine face placement on egg. Using the paintbrush, apply a thin layer of découpage medium to the egg where the face will be placed and to the back of the molded face. Attach molded face, blending edges with the paintbrush dampened with water. Let dry.

8. Pinch off pea-sized pieces of modeling compound, roll into a ball, and press into hands and feet push molds. Release molds. Let set for approximately 30 minutes.

9. To make the arms and legs, roll modeling compound into $1/2$" coils. Shape arms and legs as desired. Attach hands to arms, then attach arms to body as in Step 7 above.

10. Attach feet to legs. Do not attach legs to body at this time. Using the craft knife, miter-cut the tops of the legs to fit the shape of the body. Using a toothpick, make a hole through the mitered sections of each leg while wet. Let dry for 24 hours.

11. Using extra-fine sandpaper, lightly sand egg to smooth any blemishes in the dried modeling compound. Do not sand over facial features.

12. Finish with a light coat of acrylic varnish. Let dry.

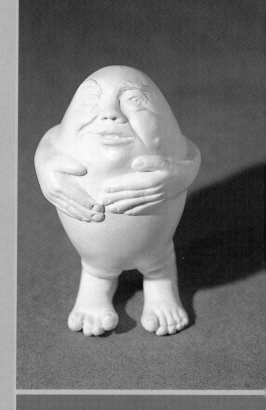

This little "egg man" is simpler to make than his cousin, Humpty Dumples, because his arms, hands, and legs are sculpted to his body.

As another option, use crackle medium and paint on his clothing to make him a conversation piece that enhances a theme focal point.

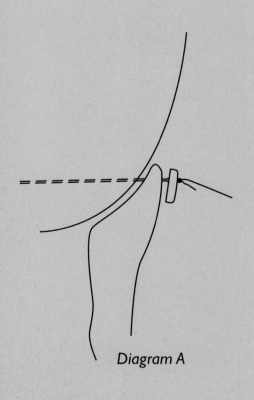

Diagram A

13. Determine leg placement on egg. Insert a doll needle into the hole in one of the legs and "scratch" a mark on the egg. Repeat on opposite side. Set legs aside. Using the needle, carefully make holes at scratch marks.

14. To attach the legs, thread the needle with a double strand of dental floss. Knot one end 3" from the end, leaving a 3" tail beyond the knot. Push threaded needle through one 2-hole button until button rests on the knot as shown in Diagram A at left. Push needle through hole in leg, through body, through remaining leg, then through remaining 2-hole button. Push needle through remaining hole in button, back through leg, through body, through leg, then through button. Firmly, but gently, pull thread taut and tie off. Trim excess floss.

15. Using the #6 round paintbrush, paint face, hands, and feet with flesh. Let dry.

16. Using a #00 round paintbrush, paint eyes with black and lips with dark pink. Let dry.

17. Using the #6 round paintbrush, apply two light coats of acrylic varnish to egg and legs. Let dry between each coat.

18. Using the Pants Pattern below, cut out one left front, one right front, one left back, and one right back from fabric.

Hint: A $\frac{1}{8}$" seam allowance is included on the pattern.

19. Place front pieces right sides together. Using a hand-sewing needle and a doubled length of thread, make small running stitches to combine front pieces. Repeat for back pieces. Place front and back right sides together. Stitch together at crotch area first, then stitch side seams. Turn right side out.

20. Fold waistband under $\frac{1}{8}$" and stitch in place. Leave a thread tail at each end so pants can be gathered at waistline. Turn hem under $\frac{1}{8}$" and stitch in place. Form pleats and stitch in place adding one 4-hole button to each leg.

21. Cut one 6" length of ribbon. Add decorative buckle to center and stitch in place. Pull thread at each side of waistline until tightly gathered and tie off. Stitch ribbon belt around top of pants. Attach a hook and eye at back and trim excess ribbon.

Design tip:

When choosing a patterned fabric such as a gingham check, make certain to choose one with a very small pattern. Otherwise, the design will be out of proportion to the egg figure.

Pants Pattern

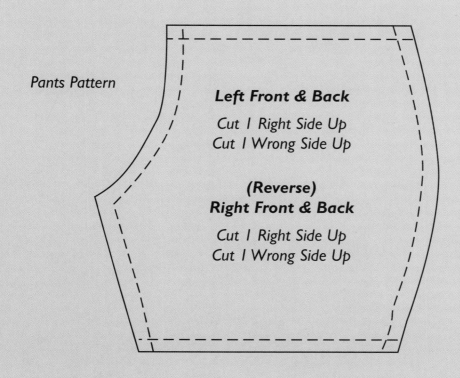

Left Front & Back

Cut 1 Right Side Up
Cut 1 Wrong Side Up

(Reverse)
Right Front & Back

Cut 1 Right Side Up
Cut 1 Wrong Side Up

all dolled up

Instructions:

1. Using scissors, cut an 8½" x 11" sheet of card stock into two 8½" x 5½" pieces.

2. To make the body, roll one piece of card stock, along the 5½" side, into a ¾"-diameter tube. Secure the edges with masking tape.

3. Stuff the body with wrapping tissue, leaving 1" space at the top of tube and ½" space at the bottom of tube.

4. Using wire cutters, cut one 13" length and one 18" length from craft wire.

5. Using a doll needle, make one hole on each side of tube approximately 1" down from top edge and ½" up from bottom edge. To make the arms, thread 13" length of wire through holes at top and bend downward. To make the legs, thread 18" length of wire through holes at bottom and bend downward.

6. Stuff tube with wrapping tissue until full.

7. To make the head, attach the wooden ball to top of body with hot glue. Make certain to tightly push the wooden ball into the glue and hold until the bond is secure.

8. Using 4" lengths of masking tape, secure wire arms to shoulders and wire legs to hips.

9. Using 12" lengths of floral tape, wrap body. Wrap arms beginning at hands and ending at shoulders. Wrap legs beginning at feet and ending at hips. Cover body, arms, and legs with a second wrap of floral tape.

List of supplies:

- Acrylic paints: metallic copper, metallic gold
- Acrylic varnish spray, satin finish
- Card stock, white, 8½" x 11" sheet
- Craft glue
- Craft wire, 18-gauge
- Découpage medium, satin finish
- Doll needle, 4"
- Embellishments
- Floral tape, white
- Florist's foil, gold
- Hand-sewing needle

(Continued on page 30)

(Continued from page 29)

- Hot-glue gun and glue sticks
- Masking tape
- Measuring spoons
- Metal ruler, 18"
- Paintbrushes: $1/2$" flat, 1" flat
- Paper ribbon, white
- Paper-twist ribbons: brown, gold
- Plastic cup
- Ribbon, $1/4$"-wide
- Scissors, sharp
- Silk leaves, autumn colors
- Thread
- Wire cutters
- Wooden ball, $1 1/2$"-diameter
- Wrapping tissue

10. Using scissors, cut five 18" lengths from paper ribbon. Lay one length of paper ribbon on a flat surface. Place an 18" metal ruler on top of the ribbon positioned 1" in from the long edge. Apply even pressure, hold ruler flat, and begin tearing ribbon against ruler with the opposite hand. Edges will be ragged and uneven. Continue across width of ribbon, tearing every 1". Continue until all five lengths have been torn into 1" strips. Set aside. Tear three of the 1" x 18" lengths of paper ribbon in half. Set aside.

11. Dilute one tablespoon découpage medium with two teaspoons water in a plastic cup. Mix well.

12. Using a $1/2$" flat paintbrush, apply mixture to one of the 9" strips of ribbon. Beginning at top of head, at approximate center of piece, drape prepared strip over the head, down to chest in front and shoulders in back. Using the paintbrush, smooth the paper ribbon giving close attention to edges and areas where head is joined to the body. Repeat until head has been completely covered with strips of paper ribbon. Let dry.

13. Repeat Step 12 above with 18" strips of ribbon until body, arms, and legs have been completely covered. Let dry.

Hint: To add definition to arms and legs, layer strips as desired.

14. To make the hair, tear $1/4$" x 3" strips of brown paper-twist ribbon. Tightly twist until ribbon begins to curl. Glue individual curls to head as desired. Let dry.

15. To make the shoes, wrap toes with tiny pieces of florist's foil and secure with craft glue.

16. Using a 1" flat paintbrush, lightly dry-brush two 24" squares of brown paper-twist ribbon with metallic copper and metallic gold. Allow to dry.

Hint: If "twist" ribbon is unavailable and paper ribbon must be substituted, the painting is easier after the ribbon has been cut into strips.

17. To make the ruffled collar, cut one 3" x 12" piece from the painted paper-twist ribbon. Cut one 3" x 12" piece from the gold paper-twist ribbon. Fold each piece in half along the 12" side. Using a hand-sewing needle and a doubled length of thread, make small running stitches along the 12" side of each piece. Tightly gather and adjust

gathers to fit around neck and shoulders. Tie off. Glue ¼"-wide ribbon around the neck, overlapping it as it is wound, until it is approximately ¾" high. Attach bottom ruffles in place with craft glue. Attach top ruffles.

18. Glue silk leaves around body as desired.

19. To make the ruffled skirt, cut one 18" x 24" piece, one 10" x 24" piece, and one 6" x 24" piece from the painted paper-twist ribbon. Cut one 14" x 24" piece and one 6" x 24" piece from the gold paper-twist ribbon. Fold each piece in half along the 24" side. Using a hand-sewing needle and a doubled length of thread, make small running stitches along the 24" side of each piece. Tightly gather and adjust gathers to fit around body at waistline. Tie off. Beginning with bottom ruffles, glue in place with craft glue. Attach each layer of ruffles in the following order from bottom to top: 9"-deep (painted), 7"-deep (gold), 5"-deep (painted), 3"-deep (gold), 3"-deep (painted). Let dry.

20. Carefully clip each ruffle in random widths around the skirt, starting from the bottom edge up to where it has been glued. Using your fingers, gently open up each section of ruffles as if it were a balloon curtain.

Hint: Nothing needs to be stuffed inside the ruffles because the strength and durability of the ribbon will hold its own shape.

21. Embellish as desired.

22. Spray with two light coats of acrylic varnish. Let dry between each coat.

japanese kimonos

in harmony

List of supplies:

- Acrylic paints:
  light and dark shades
  of same color

- Acrylic varnish,
  satin finish

- Baking dish,
  9" x 12" x 2"

- Ballpoint pen

- Blender

- Cornstarch

- Craft foam, ¹/₄"-thick

(Continued on page 33)

Instructions:

1. To make the papier-mâché pulp, soak egg carton overnight in a 12-quart plastic dishpan filled with cool water. Tear into postage-stamp-sized pieces.

2. Fill a blender container ²/₃ full of cool water. Add ¹/₄ cup of torn egg carton pieces. Pulse blender several times, then blend at high speed for approximately 25 seconds. Place blended pulp in the plastic dishpan. Repeat until plastic dishpan is half full of blended pulp. Add two quarts cool water and stir with your hand. Set aside.

3. Using a pencil, trace Kimono Pattern from page 35 onto plain paper. Using scissors, cut shape from paper.

4. Place shape in the center of a piece of craft foam. Adhere in place with masking tape. Trace around shape with a ballpoint pen. Remove pattern.

5. Place craft foam on a cutting mat. Using a craft knife, carefully cut out shape.

Hint: The shape that "falls out" will be set aside and used only to help protect the mold pattern while it is in storage.

6. Place both nylon tulle squares in an embroidery hoop making certain surface is tight.

7. Place embroidery hoop, netting side up, on the bottom of a baking dish. Place craft foam with cut-out shape at center of hoop, resting on the netting.

(Continued from page 32)

- Craft knife, sharp
- Creative Paperclay® modeling compound, white, 3 oz.
- Cutting mat
- Decorative buttons, assorted shapes and sizes
- Découpage medium, satin finish
- Disposable cup
- Doll needle, 4"
- Egg carton, paper
- Embroidery floss
- Embroidery hoop, 8"-round
- Glazing medium, clear
- Masking tape
- Measuring cups
- Measuring spoons
- Nylon tulle, 12"-square (2)
- Paintbrushes: 1/4" flat, #6 round
- Paper towels
- Plastic dishpan, 12-quart
- Polymer clay
- Scissors, sharp
- Sheet sponge
- Tracing paper
- Wooden pencil

8. Stir the blended pulp and water mixture. Using a 1-cup measuring cup with pouring spout, fill $1/2$ to $2/3$ full of pulp and slowly pour into kimono shape, allowing the water to drain through the netting into the pan.

Hint: Pour pulp as evenly as possible.

9. When pulp reaches depth of craft foam, lay a folded paper towel and a piece of sheet sponge on the pulp to remove excess moisture. Squeeze the sponge dry and repeat.

10. Using a $1/4$" flat paintbrush, move excess pulp from edges of craft foam into kimono shape. Continue working across shape with paintbrush, pushing pulp against netting to remove water and to add texture.

Hint: Water may be poured out of baking dish as necessary.

11. Repeat Steps 8–10 above until three cups of pulp have been poured into kimono shape.

12. To remove molded kimono, use the paintbrush to push edges away from the craft foam. Lay the wet shape on a layer of paper towels.

Hint: Pour the number of kimonos as desired. Discard excess pulp by flushing down the toilet.

13. To make the embossed design, begin by making the mold. To do this, pinch off one walnut-sized piece of polymer clay, roll into a ball, and slightly press to flatten until it is approximately $1/4$" thick. Using a

Brass charms with an Asian theme can be glued or wired to these kimono shapes. Tiny tassels, purchased or handmade, can also be added for interest.

dry paintbrush, dust decorative part of button and top of clay with cornstarch. Press the button into the clay, then carefully remove. Bake the mold according to manufacturer's instructions. Let cool.

14. Dust inside of mold with cornstarch.

15. Pinch off pea-sized pieces of modeling compound, roll into balls, and press into mold.

16. While the embossed design and the kimono are still wet, apply découpage medium to the back of the embossed design. Carefully place on kimono, positioned at the center of the shoulders. Gently press the design into the wet pulp. Let dry.

Hint: If necessary, small bits of pulp may be lifted from the baking dish and placed at the rim of the design with the paintbrush to help seal the edges.

17. Using the paintbrush, apply two light coats of acrylic varnish to both sides of kimono. Let dry between each coat.

18. Using a #6 round paintbrush, paint both sides of kimono. Begin with darkest shade of color at top and lightest shade of color at bottom, brushing to mix shades at the center. Let dry.

19. Mix one teaspoon white pearl paint and one teaspoon glazing medium in a disposable cup. Add three drops of water and mix. Using the paintbrush, paint both sides of kimono. Let dry.

20. Using a $1/2$" flat paintbrush, dry-brush areas of high texture with metallic gold. Let dry.

21. Using a doll needle, make one hole at each shoulder. To make the hanger, thread embroidery floss through the holes and knot at each shoulder.

Design tips:

A softer, more paper-like texture can be created by using less pulp when pouring the shape.

For kimonos made for any festive Oriental celebration, try adding glitter to the pulp during the mixing stage.

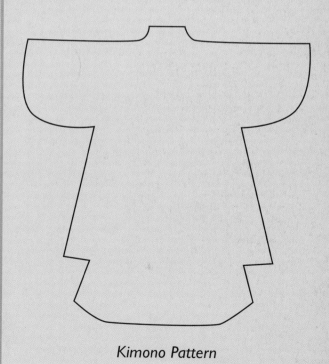

Kimono Pattern

List of supplies:

- Acrylic paint, flesh
- Acrylic varnish spray, satin finish
- Cotton swab
- Craft glue
- Craft wire, 20-gauge
- Decorative beads
- Découpage medium, satin finish
- Dressmaker's pin
- Floral tape, white
- Hand-sewing needle
- Japanese Yuzen origami paper, patterned
- Monofilament thread
- Paintbrush, #6 round
- Paper parasol
- Plastic cup
- Scissors, sharp
- Thread
- Toothpick
- Wire cutters
- Wooden pencil, round, unsharpened
- Wrapping tissues: green, white

spring rain doll

:ructions:

1. Using wire cutters, cut one 23" length from 20-gauge wire.

2. Bend the wire into a free-form figure as shown in Diagram A at lower right.

3. Using wire cutters, clip cotton tip from a cotton swab. To make the head, attach the cotton tip inside the wire loop with craft glue.

4. Using 12" lengths of floral tape, wrap body. Wrap arms beginning at hands and ending at shoulders. Wrap legs beginning at feet and ending at hips. Cover body, arms, and legs with a second wrap of floral tape.

5. Using scissors, cut several $1/4$" x 18" strips from white wrapping tissue. Set aside.

6. Dilute one tablespoon découpage medium with two teaspoons water in a plastic cup. Mix well.

7. Using a paintbrush, apply mixture to head area. Beginning at top of head, wrap strips around the head as if it were a mummy. Repeat until head is the desired size and has been completely covered with strips of wrapping tissue. Let dry.

8. Repeat Step 7 above with $1/4$" x 12" strips of wrapping tissue until body, arms, and legs have been completely covered.

Hint: To add definition to arms and legs, layer strips as desired.

9. Bend arms and legs into desired position. Let dry to touch.

10. Using the paintbrush, paint entire figure with two coats of flesh. Let dry between each coat.

11. To make the shoes, place a tiny piece of green wrapping tissue on each foot and secure with découpage medium. Repeat for panties.

12. Using the paintbrush, apply two light coats of découpage medium to entire figure. Let dry between each coat.

13. Tightly, but gently, crumple a 6" square of origami paper. Smooth the wrinkles and place on a flat surface. To crimp the paper, lightly roll it around an unsharpened pencil. Hold the unsharpened end of the pencil perpendicular to the table and firmly push the paper downward. Remove and smooth. Repeat, working from top to bottom and from side to side. Roll and crimp edges and shape with fingers.

Design tip:

It is important to bend figure into desired position while paper and découpage medium are pliable. Once they have completely dried, approximately eight to ten hours, they become rigid.

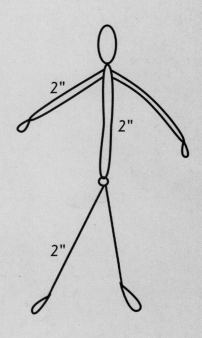

Diagram A

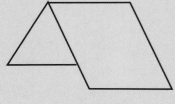

Diagram B

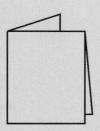

Diagram C

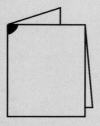

Diagram D

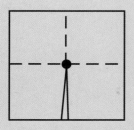

Diagram E

14. Flatten and smooth paper. Cut three 2" x 6" rectangles. To make the bodice, trim one of the rectangles to 2" x 4". Fold this rectangle in half to form a 2" square as shown in Diagram B at left. Holding the folded edge at top of square, fold again from side to side as shown in Diagram C at left.

15. To form the opening for the neck, cut the tip off the four-point fold in a rounded manner as shown in Diagram D at left. Open folded shape and cut from bottom cut edge to opening for neck along the fold as shown in Diagram E at left. Refold.

16. To form the sleeves and shape the bodice, cut a ¹/₄" x 1" rectangle from the shape as shown in Diagram F on page 39.

17. Cut a ¹/₈" diagonal slit under each sleeve as shown in Diagram G on page 39. Unfold and flatten bodice shape with right side of paper facing up. Fold ¹/₈" seams under at sides of bodice and under sleeves. Using a toothpick, apply craft glue to seams and press together.

18. To make the skirt, join the remaining two 2" x 6" rectangles into a single strip by gluing ¹/₈" at the joining 2" edge. Smooth and flatten seam. Let dry.

19. Place strip patterned side down. Turn bottom long edge up ¹/₄" to form the hemline.

20. To make the lining for the skirt, turn bottom long edge of a 2" x 12" strip of green wrapping tissue up ¹/₄". Glue wrapping tissue to the wrong side of the skirt with craft glue, matching hemlines. Trim excess off edges. Let dry. Repeat Step 13 on page 37.

21. Using a hand-sewing needle and a doubled length of thread, make small running stitches along the top edge approximately ¹/₄" down. Tightly gather and adjust gathers to fit around waist. Tie off.

22. Place bodice on figure, gluing seam at front with craft glue. Beginning at gathered edge of skirt, glue skirt around waist. Let dry.

Hint: It may be necessary to reposition the arms so the dress is not stressed or torn, then return arms to their original positions.

23. To make the bandana, cut a 2" equilateral triangle from origami paper. Attach to head with craft glue.

24. Open a paper parasol. Using the paintbrush, apply a light coat of découpage medium to paper "ribs." Let dry. Repeat three times, applying a light coat each time.

Hint: If too much découpage medium is applied at the beginning, the ribs will soak up the moisture and the parasol will collapse in on itself.

25. Attach parasol to doll's hand with craft glue.

26. To make the hanger, double a length of monofilament thread and knot the ends together to make a loop for hanging. Using a dressmaker's pin, attach to top center of head.

27. To make the sash, tightly gather a $1/2$" x 4" strip of green wrapping tissue. Tie off. Twist to form flowers and attach around waistline with craft glue. Add a decorative bead at the center of each flower.

28. Spray with three light coats of acrylic varnish. Let dry between each coat.

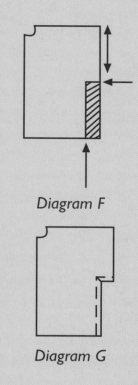

Diagram F

Diagram G

Design tip:

Use portions of the parasol pleated paper to make the fan options as shown at left.

Several of these dolls could be made and attached to wire hangers for a mobile. Each doll could be made from a variety of colorful patterned origami papers.

lapel ladies

List of supplies:

- Cotton swab
- Craft glue
- Craft wire, 20-gauge
- Découpage medium, satin finish
- Embellishments
- Industrial-strength adhesive
- Measuring spoons
- Paintbrush, #6 round
- Pin backs, $^3/_4$"-long
- Plastic cup
- Scissors, sharp
- Silk-paper napkin
- Metallic thread, fine
- Wire cutters
- Wrapping tissue, white

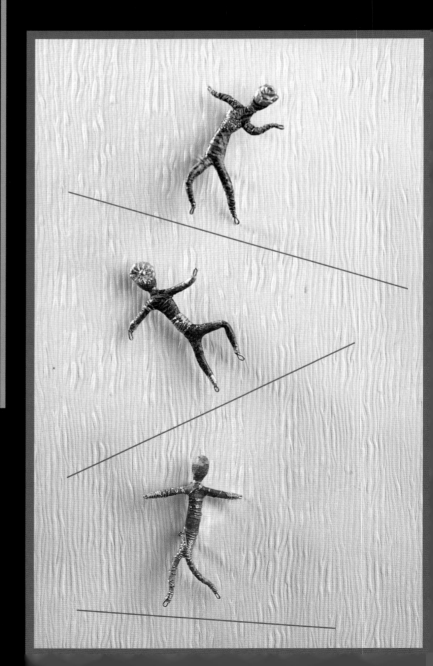

Instructions:

1. Using wire cutters, cut one 10" length from 20-gauge wire for each figure desired.

2. Bend the wire into a free-form figure as shown in Diagram A on page 37. Recalculate the proportional dimensions so figure is approximately 3" tall.

3. Using wire cutters, clip cotton tip from a cotton swab. To make the head, attach the cotton tip inside the wire loop with craft glue.

4. Using scissors, cut several ¹/₄" x 10" strips of white wrapping tissue. Set aside.

5. Dilute one tablespoon découpage medium with two teaspoons water in a plastic cup. Mix well.

6. Using a paintbrush, apply mixture to head area. Beginning at top of head, wrap strips around the head as if it were a mummy. Repeat until head is the desired size and has been completely covered with strips of wrapping tissue. Let dry.

7. Repeat Step 6 above with ¹/₄" x10" strips of wrapping tissue until body, arms, and legs have been completely covered. Wrap arms beginning at wrists and ending at shoulders. Wrap legs beginning at ankles and ending at hips.

Hint: To add definition to arms and legs, layer strips as desired.

8. Repeat Steps 4–7 above, using strips of silk-paper napkin.

Hint: Repeat gluing and wrapping until the desired depth of color is achieved in layers.

9. Bend arms and legs into desired position. Let dry.

10. Using the paintbrush, apply five light coats of découpage medium to entire figure. Let dry between each coat.

11. Randomly bind figure at ankles, wrists, and waist with coordinating or contrasting metallic thread. Secure the ends with craft glue.

12. Attach pin backs to the back side of each figure with industrial-strength adhesive.

13. Embellish as desired.

Because of their translucent quality, "silk-paper" napkins show color through each succeeding layer. Their patterns become indistinct as more layers are added.

41

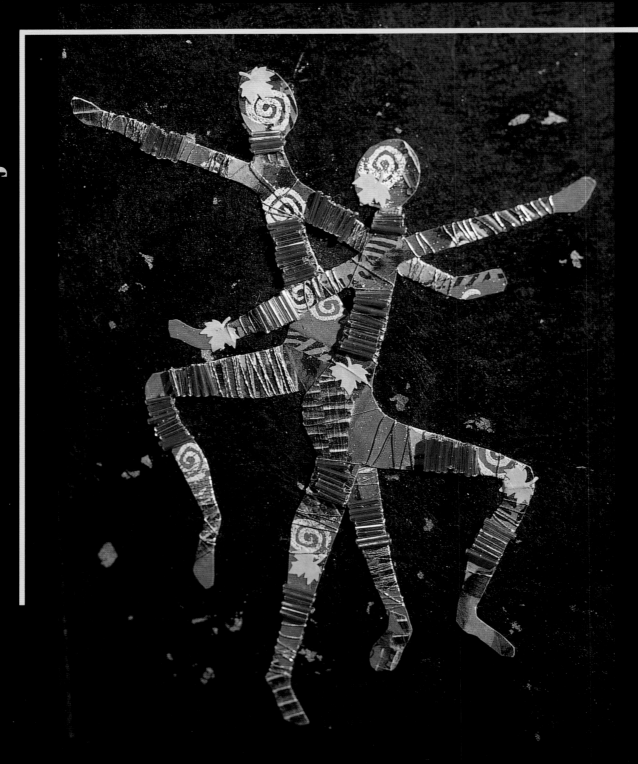

the last word

Instructions:

1. Tear a variety of patterned papers into postage-stamp-sized pieces.

2. Using a $1/2$" flat paintbrush, apply nonwrinkling paper glue to wrong sides of torn paper pieces, then press onto heavy card stock. Repeat until card stock is completely covered.

3. Place card stock between sheets of waxed paper and press under weights for 24 hours to flatten.

4. Using a pencil, trace Tribal Dancer Pattern from page 45 onto plain paper. Using scissors, cut shape from paper.

5. Position template on paper-covered card stock and secure in place with masking tape.

Hint: Make certain to position template so a second figure can be cut from the same piece of card stock.

6. Trace around shape with fiber-tip pen. Remove template and re-position on card stock as in Step 5 above. Trace around second shape and remove template.

Hint: Turn template over so each dancer faces the opposite direction.

7. Cut dancers from card stock.

8. Secure any loose edges of paper onto card stock with paper glue.

9. Using a small spiral rubber stamp and a heat gun, randomly emboss spirals on dancers with embossing ink and yellow-gold embossing powder.

10. Using a small maple-leaf-shaped paper punch, punch out numerous leaves from gold card stock. Randomly adhere to dancers.

List of supplies:

- Beading wire
- Bugle beads, assorted colors
- Card stock, gold, $8^1/2$" x 11" sheet
- Card stock, heavy, $8^1/2$" x 11" sheet
- Découpage medium, satin finish
- Embossing ink
- Embossing powder, yellow-gold
- Fiber-tip pen, ultrafine
- Hand towel
- Heat gun
- Journal
- Masking tape
- Metallic thread, fine
- Nonwrinkling paper glue

(Continued on page 44)

(Continued from page 43)

- Paintbrushes:
  $^1/_2$" flat, #6 round

- Paper punch,
  small maple leaf

- Patterned papers

- Plain paper

- Rubber stamp,
  small spiral

- Scissors, sharp

- Transparent tape

- Waxed paper

- Wooden pencil

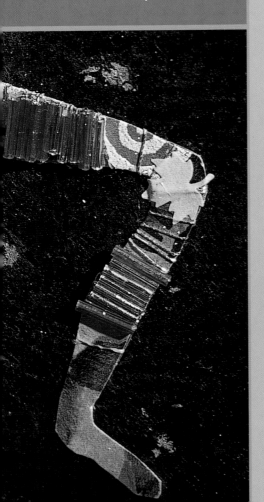

11. Secure a single strand of metallic gold thread at back of one dancer's head with transparent tape. Wrap thread around dancer, clustering and crossing threads over each other. Secure at back of dancer with transparent tape. Repeat for remaining dancer.

12. Cut beading wire into twelve 14" lengths.

13. Slide one bugle bead onto one length of wire. Position it at center and secure by twisting bead two times.

14. Hold bead in place horizontally at front of dancer's neck. Carry wires to back of neck and twist. Bring one end of wire from back of neck to front of neck.

15. Slide one bugle bead onto wire and position it horizontally under first bead. Carry wire to back of neck and twist wires together. Bring opposite end of wire from back of neck to front of neck.

16. Slide one bugle bead onto wire and position it horizontally under second bead. Repeat until you have the desired number of beads around neck. Repeat for remaining dancer.

17. Randomly add series of bugle beads, horizontally positioned, on dancer, such as at forearms, thighs, calves, and bodices, as in Steps 13–16 above. Repeat for remaining dancer.

18. Using a #6 round paintbrush, apply a light coat of découpage medium to backs of dancers. Let dry. Repeat two times making certain the découpage medium is worked between the wires.

19. Determine placement on cover of journal. Apply a generous layer of découpage medium to backs of dancers. Arrange on journal as desired.

20. Cover with a sheet of waxed paper, then with a folded hand towel. Press under weights for 24 hours to flatten. Remove hand towel and waxed paper. Press under weights for an additional 24 hours.

Tribal Dancer Pattern

Design tip:

To enhance the cover of the journal, it can be covered with a piece of Oriental lace paper. Apply a coat of découpage medium to the surface, then place a piece of lace paper on top of it. Using a paintbrush, gently brush the paper into the découpage medium, working from the center to the outside edges. Let dry. Apply a second coat and allow to dry.

starlight wizard

List of supplies:

- Acrylic paints: black, royal blue, flesh, metallic gold, pink, white, white pearl

- Acrylic varnish, satin finish

- Bamboo skewer

- Card stock, heavy, 11" x 14"

- Cellulose powder

- Cornstarch

- Craft glue

- Craft knife, sharp

- Creative Paperclay® modeling compound, white, 3 oz.

- Découpage medium, satin finish

- Disposable cup

- Embellishments

- Florist's foil, gold

- Glazing medium, clear

- Measuring spoons

- Mixing bowl, large

- Mohair

- Paintbrush, #6 round

(Continued on page 47)

Instructions:

1. Using a dry paintbrush, dust inside of push molds with cornstarch.

2. Pinch off pea-sized pieces of modeling compound, roll into a ball, and press into face push mold. Release mold. Let set for approximately 30 minutes.

3. Using a craft knife, carefully trim excess modeling compound from back of molded face until it is approximately ¹/₂" thick.

4. Pinch off pea-sized pieces of modeling compound, roll into a ball, and press into hands push molds. Release molds. Let set for approximately 30 minutes.

5. Roll card stock into cone shape. Secure at seam line with transparent tape.

6. Using scissors, trim around bottom edge of cone to adjust height.

7. Make the papier-mâché pulp as with Pinecone Santa, Steps 1–4, on page 17.

8. Place a paper towel flat on a rigid surface. Place a walnut-sized piece of papier-mâché on the paper towel and flatten until it is approximately ¹/₄" thick. Remove papier-mâché from the paper towel and wrap around the cone. Smooth with fingers, smoothing and blending as necessary. Let dry for 24 hours.

Hint: If too much moisture or weight is added to the cone too quickly, it will collapse.

9. Make the sleeves from papier-mâché and attach to robe.

10. Using the paintbrush, apply a thin layer of découpage medium to the top of the cone where the face will be placed and to the back of the molded face. Attach molded face, blending edges with the paintbrush dampened with water. Let dry.

11. Place hands in sleeves and attach as in Step 10 above.

12. Roll papier-mâché into a ¹/₄" coil. Shape around face as desired. To make the hood, add additional papier-mâché to top of cone and shape as desired.

13. Roll papier-mâché into two ¹/₄" coils. Shape around sleeves to make cuffs as desired. Fill in around hands with papier-mâché.

(Continued from page 46)

- Paper punch, small star
- Paper towels
- Plastic dishpan, 12-quart
- Push molds: face, hands
- Scissors, sharp
- Sieve, fine
- Spray glitter, ultrafine, opalescent
- Table fork
- Toilet paper, 2-ply, 1 roll
- Toothpick, round
- Transparent tape
- Wire whisk

Pulp-type papier-mâché, whether purchased or homemade, dries to a bumpy, dimpled texture. It can be smoothed somewhat by laying small pieces of plastic wrap over the wet surface and gently rubbing with your finger. The plastic wrap must remain on the surface of the pulp until it is dry.

Note: Wrapping will slow the drying process and there is a possibility of mold forming in more humid climates. Good air circulation is helpful.

14. Using a toothpick, make a hole through both hands to accommodate magic wand.

15. Roll papier-mâché into a ¹/₂" coil. Place down center of gown where both sides would meet.

16. Roll papier-mâché into a 1" coil. Flute around hemline of gown. Allow to dry.

17. Using the paintbrush, paint face and hands with flesh, eyes with black, eyebrows with white, and cheeks and lips with pink. Let dry.

18. Paint robe with two coats of royal blue paint. Let dry between each coat.

19. Mix equal parts of royal blue paint, white pearl paint, and glazing medium in a disposable cup. Using the paintbrush, paint robe.

20. While still wet, stipple hood area around face, sleeve cuffs, and hemline of robe with white pearl paint, blending light areas into dark areas. Let dry.

21. Using a small star-shaped paper punch, punch out numerous stars from florist's foil. Randomly adhere to robe with craft glue.

22. Using the paintbrush, apply two light coats of acrylic varnish to all papier-mâché areas. Let dry between each coat.

23. To make the beard, adhere a thin "tuft" of mohair fibers to chin.

24. To make the magic wand, cut a 4" length from a bamboo skewer. Paint with two coats of metallic gold. Let dry. Fold a piece of card stock in half and cut two identical stars. Separate the star shapes, spread a thin layer of craft glue on one side of each star, place the painted length of bamboo skewer on one star, and position the remaining star on top in perfect alignment. Let dry.

25. Paint both sides of star with two coats of metallic gold. Let dry.

26. Embellish wizard and magic wand as desired.

27. Place magic wand through the hole in hands and secure with craft glue.

28. Spray with two light coats of opalescent glitter. Let dry between each coat.

win, lose, love

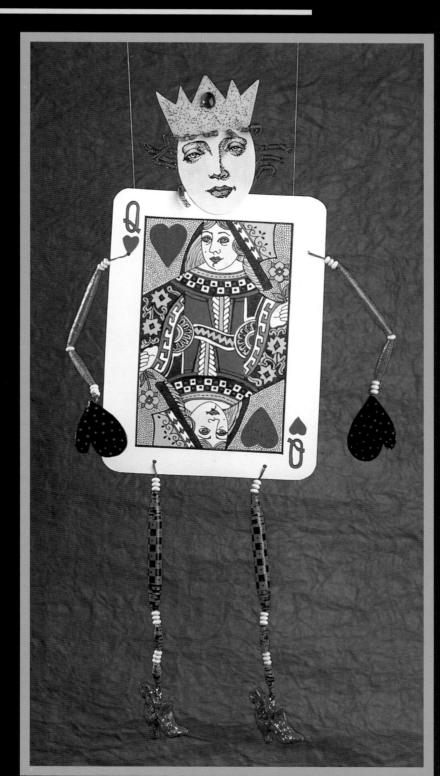

List of supplies:

- Acrylic paints:
  blue, flesh,
  pale pink, red
- Bamboo skewer
- Brass charm,
  $2\frac{1}{2}$" Victorian shoe
- Cabochon, $\frac{1}{2}$", red
- Card stocks, heavy:
  black, yellow
- Cornstarch
- Craft glue
- Craft wire,
  18-gauge, red
- Creative Paperclay® modeling compound, white, 3 oz.
- Deck of playing cards, standard size
- Découpage medium, satin finish
- Embossing powder, black
- Fusible web, lightweight
- Glitter paint, red
- Heat gun
- Iron
- Jump rings (2)

(Continued on page 51)

Instructions:

1. Make a black-and-white photocopy, enlarged to 220%, of the queen of hearts playing card.

2. Secure to the underside of an 8" x 10" piece of watercolor paper with masking tape.

3. Using a light-box or holding up to a window, trace the design with a #3 pencil. Remove masking tape and photocopy.

4. Using scissors, cut out card, leaving a 1" border on top, bottom, and each side. Round corners.

5. Using a black marker, go over pencil lines.

6. Using a #2 round paintbrush, paint areas of color on card with diluted acrylic paints. Let dry.

Hint: Use the original playing card for color reference.

7. Draw and paint the "Q" and heart in upper-left and bottom-right corners with red and black markers.

8. Using an iron and fusible web, bond a piece of watercolor paper to the back of the card.

Hint: Use a pressing cloth to avoid stray marks on watercolor paper.

9. Cut around watercolor paper so back card matches up to front card perfectly.

10. Using a natural or synthetic sponge, randomly sponge-paint back of card with red paint.

11. Paint large hearts within the black border with red glitter paint. Seal hearts with three light coats of découpage medium. Let dry between each coat.

12. Using a $\frac{1}{16}$" round paper punch, punch holes at sides and bottom of card to accommodate wires for arms and legs.

13. From one patterned paper, cut two triangles $2\frac{1}{2}$" wide at the base x 7" long at the sides and two triangles $1\frac{1}{4}$" wide x 7" long. From the remaining patterned paper, cut two triangles 4" wide x $8\frac{1}{2}$" long and four triangles 1" wide x $8\frac{1}{2}$" long.

14. To make the paper beads for the arms and legs, wind each triangular-shaped paper piece onto a bamboo skewer, beginning at the base of each triangle. Roll two or three times around the skewer, then secure with a drop of craft glue. Continue rolling firmly, but not so tightly that the "bead" will not slip off the skewer. Secure at ends with a drop of craft glue. Using a #6 round paintbrush, apply two coats of découpage medium to each of the beads. Let dry between each coat.

15. Using the Mitten Pattern on page 52, cut out four mittens from black card stock.

16. Using wire cutters, cut six 12" lengths from craft wire. Working with three of the lengths, thread wires through hole at one side of card to make an arm. Twist wires twice to secure. Thread three wooden beads onto wire and push upward so top bead touches edge of card. Add one $2^1/_2$" long paper bead, one wooden bead, one $1^1/_4$" long paper bead, and three wooden beads. Twist wires three times to secure. Repeat for opposite arm.

17. To attach the mitten at the end of each arm, place two of the shapes together so they match perfectly. Place the wire ends in between the shapes and secure in place with craft glue. Repeat for remaining mitten.

18. Repeat Step 16 above to make each leg, cutting six 18" lengths from craft wire. Thread three wooden beads onto wire and push upward so top bead touches edge of card. Add one 4" long paper bead, three wooden beads, one 1" long paper bead, three wooden beads, and one 1" long paper bead. Form a loop from the three strands of wire and push the ends back up into the last paper bead.

19. Using needle-nosed pliers, attach one jump ring to the loop at the bottom of each leg.

20. To make the shoes, dust inside of brass charm with cornstarch, using a dry paintbrush.

21. Pinch off pea-sized pieces of modeling compound, roll into a ball, and press into brass charm. Release mold. Smooth edges and back side of shoe. Repeat for remaining shoe.

(Continued from page 50)

- Light-box
- Masking tape
- Needle-nosed pliers
- Paintbrushes:
  #2 round, #6 round
- Paper punch,
  $^1/_{16}$" round
- Patterned papers:
  2 designs
- Permanent markers:
  .05 extra-fine-tip, black;
  1.0 fine-tip,
  assorted colors
- Pigment ink, black
- Rubber stamp,
  face
- Scissors, sharp
- Screw eyes, 5mm (2)
- Sponge
- Stylus
- Template, oval size,
  $2^1/_4$"-wide x $3^1/_4$"-high
- Transparent tape
- Watercolor paper
- Wire cutters
- Wooden beads (32)
- Wooden pencil,
  #3 medium-hard

Mitten Pattern

Hint: This figure will have two left feet since both shoes are made from the same mold.

22. Using the paintbrush, apply two light coats of découpage medium to the shoes. Let dry between each coat.

23. Using the #2 round paintbrush, apply two coats of red paint and two coats of red glitter paint to both sides of shoes. Let dry between each coat.

24. Screw the screw eyes into shoes at upper edge.

25. Using the #6 round paintbrush, apply three coats of découpage medium. Let dry between each coat.

26. Using a rubber stamp and black pigment ink, stamp a face onto watercolor paper. Using a heat gun, emboss face with black embossing powder.

27. Using an oval template and a pencil, draw an oval around face. Using scissors, cut out oval. Place it back on the watercolor paper and cut out a second oval.

28. Using the paintbrush, paint face with flesh paint, eyelids with blue, and lips with red. Blush cheeks with pale pink. Let dry.

29. Using a stylus, add dots randomly on both sides of mittens with red. Let dry. Using the paintbrush, apply two light coats of découpage medium to red dots. Let dry between each coat.

30. Using the Queen's Crown Pattern on page 53, cut out two crowns from yellow card stock.

31. Using the paintbrush, apply a light coat of red glitter paint to one side of one crown. Let dry. Apply two light coats of découpage medium to red glitter paint. Let dry between each coat.

32. To make the hair, wind various lengths of craft wire around the bamboo skewer. Remove wires and stretch at the centers leaving "curls" on each end. Secure stretched area of the wires to the back of the oval that has the face embossed on it with transparent tape.

Hint: Placement of these wires should be approximately at the center.

33. Spread a thin layer of craft glue over the tape, wires, and back side of oval. Place the two ovals together so they match perfectly. Press around all outside edges. Gently lift area at chin and affix head to body, sandwiching the card between and two ovals. Press together. Let dry.

34. Repeat Step 32 on page 52, securing the stretched wires to back of crown. Repeat Step 33 above, affixing crown to head. Allow to dry.

35. Adhere cabochon to top center of crown with craft glue.

Queen's Crown Pattern

dream catcher

List of supplies:

- Acrylic paints: metallic bronze, burgundy, metallic copper, metallic gold

- Beading wire, metallic gold

- Cheesecloth

- Cornstarch

- Crackle medium, ultrafine

- Craft glue

- Creative Paperclay® modeling compound, white, 3 oz.

- Découpage medium, satin finish

- Handmade paper

- Linen craft thread

- Paintbrush, #6 round

- Paper towels

- Pebbles, small flat

- Push mold, face

- Scissors, sharp

- Twigs, $1/4$"-diameter

- Wrapping tissue, metallic gold

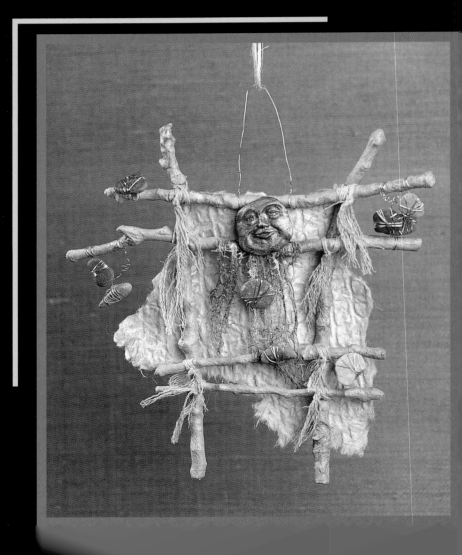

Instructions:

1. Using scissors, cut several $1/2$" x 10" strips from wrapping tissue. Using a paintbrush, apply a coat of découpage medium to the strips of wrapping tissue. Wrap each twig with two layers of wrapping tissue. Let dry.

2. Lay twigs out as shown in Diagram A at right and adhere at joints with craft glue. Let dry. Bind joints with linen craft thread. Tie a knot at each joint and leave $1^3/4$" tails. To make the tassels, fray the tails of the thread.

3. Cut one 2" x 4" piece from cheesecloth and fray one 2" edge. Using the paintbrush, paint both sides of cheesecloth with two generous coats of metallic gold paint. Let dry between each coat.

4. Adhere cheesecloth to horizontal twig at center of figure with craft glue.

5. Using a dry paintbrush, dust inside of push mold with cornstarch.

6. Pinch off pea-sized pieces of modeling compound, roll into a ball, and press into face push mold. Release mold.

7. Using the paintbrush, apply two coats of découpage medium to both sides of face. Let dry between each coat.

8. Paint face with equal parts of metallic bronze and metallic copper paint. Let dry.

9. Apply a light coat of crackle medium to face. Let dry. Brush over surface with burgundy paint until entire face has crackled surface. Dip paintbrush in water and "scrub" paint into the cracks that were made by the crackle medium.

10. Gently wipe with a damp paper towel to remove excess paint. Let dry. Apply a light coat of découpage medium. Let dry.

11. Adhere face to horizontal twig at top of figure with craft glue.

12. Wind various lengths of beading wire around small pebbles, then randomly attach to twigs and cheesecloth.

13. Tear a piece of handmade paper into an asymmetrical shape. Glue it to the back of the twig form.

14. To make the hanger, attach a length of beading wire in two places at center of twig at top to make a loop for hanging.

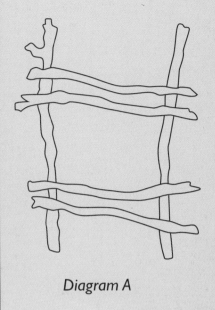

Diagram A

Design tip:

Try making this dream catcher in a circular shape by attaching the wrapped twigs around a metal ring or embroidery hoop. Additional twigs can then be added across the diameter of the circular shape.

an artist's touch

List of supplies:

- *Blending stump*
- *Color photograph*
- *Colored pencils, artist's quality, assorted colors*
- *Craft knife, sharp*
- *Masking tape*
- *Scissors, sharp*
- *Solvent-based liquid colorless marker*
- *Watercolor paper, lightweight, smooth*

modern kids

Instructions:

1. Make a color photocopy, with the image reversed, of a photograph. Enlarge as desired.

Hint: Commercial-quality color copiers have a special type of ink. Do not use a desktop or home copier.

2. Using scissors, trim excess background from around figure, leaving approximately a 1" margin on all sides.

3. Working on a flat surface, place photocopy face down on watercolor paper. Secure with masking tape.

4. Using a solvent-based colorless marker, begin coloring over the areas to be transferred. Cap the marker, then firmly rub over saturated area with a blending stump. Continue until entire figure has been transferred onto the watercolor paper.

Hint: Apply to small areas, approximately 2" square or smaller.

5. Carefully remove tape at one area to check the quality of the transfer. The image should have an "antique" or "ghostlike" appearance; however, enough detail should have transferred to define where colored-pencil enhancement will be added.

Hint: If some areas need more definition, reapply solvent and rub again, using caution not to "shift" the image.

6. Remove tape. Let watercolor paper image air-dry. Discard used photocopy.

7. To color the image, color in faces, arms, and legs with flesh-colored pencil. Blush cheeks and lips with pink. Color hair and clothing with colors that match as closely as possible.

Hint: Working lightly and applying colors in layers gives more control.

8. Cut figure from watercolor paper, trimming away all of the background. For areas that are enclosed, such as between the arms and the body, a craft knife can be used.

Design tips:

These figures can be used in a number of ways. Try the following:

- Use them on scrapbook pages.

- Use them as gift tags.

- Create an ornament as on page 10, by using one of your favorite photographs substituted for the angel art image.

- Make your own greeting cards.

- Images can be glued to foam-core board, then carefully cut out with a craft knife. Finish edges and back with acrylic paint. An easel back can be added if you want figures to stand.

colonial damsel

& sensibility

Instructions:

1. Make a color photocopy, with the image reversed, of a reproduction Colonial art image. Enlarge to 8¹/₂" x 10".

Hint: Commercial-quality color copiers have a special type of ink. Do not use a desktop or home copier.

2. Continue as with Modern Kids, Steps 3–7, on page 57, but do not cut figure from the watercolor paper.

3. Determine placement of ribbonwork. Arrange ribbon as desired.

Hint: Wire-edged ribbon is the best choice of ribbon for this project because it can be folded and gathered and will maintain its shape.

4. Using scissors, cut ribbon to the appropriate length plus ¹/₂" on each end.

5. Using a craft knife, make slits in the watercolor paper. Using the tip of a table knife, gently work the raw edges of the ribbon through the slits in the watercolor paper. Secure excess ribbon on the back side of the watercolor paper with masking tape.

6. Repeat Steps 3–5 above until all ribbonwork has been completed.

7. Using a hand-sewing needle and a doubled length of thread, stitch small embellishments onto watercolor paper.

8. Mat and frame as desired.

Hint: The resulting art could be used optionally as an album cover, a section for a lamp shade, or to embellish the top of a hat or band box.

List of supplies:

- Blending stump
- Colored pencils, artist's quality, assorted colors
- Craft knife, sharp
- Embellishments, small
- Frame
- Hand-sewing needle
- Masking tape
- Mat
- Reproduction Colonial art image
- Ribbon, wire-edged
- Scissors, sharp
- Solvent-based liquid colorless marker
- Table knife
- Thread
- Watercolor paper, lightweight, smooth

List of supplies:

- Acrylic paints:
  dark brown,
  deep reddish brown,
  rust, tan

- Bamboo skewer

- Copper leaf

- Cornstarch

- Craft glue

- Creative Paperclay® modeling compound,
  white, 3 oz.

- Découpage medium,
  satin finish

- Disposable cup

- Fabric paint,
  metallic gold

- Gold leaf

- Hot-glue gun and
  glue sticks

- Japanese paper,
  heavy-weight,
  8" x 10"

(Continued on page 61)

leaf man

60

Instructions:

1. Fold a piece of Japanese paper in half to measure 8" x 5". Unfold and flatten.

2. Using a large decorative leaf rubber stamp and brown pigment ink, stamp a leaf onto one side of the folded paper. Let dry.

3. Using a paint applicator, outline all leaf veins with metallic gold fabric paint. Let dry.

4. Mix two drops of tan paint and two teaspoons of water in a disposable cup. Using a #6 round paintbrush, paint the stamped leaf in a random pattern until completely covered. While leaf is still wet, repeat with rust paint and with dark brown paint.

Hint: Make certain to leave areas of all colors showing.

5. Rinse paintbrush and gently brush over leaf veins to remove excess paint. Let dry.

6. For back leaf, repeat Step 4 above on the remaining half of the folded paper. Let dry.

7. Using scissors, cut paper in half along the fold line. Holding papers together, painted sides out, cut around stamped leaf. You will have two perfectly matched leaves.

(Continued from page 60)

- Paint applicator, ultrafine tip
- Paintbrush, #6 round
- Pigment ink, brown
- Polyester stuffing
- Push mold, face
- Reindeer moss
- Rubber stamp, large decorative leaf
- Scissors, sharp
- Spoon
- Twigs, $1/4$"-diameter, $3 1/2$"-long (5)

Design tip:

Commercially purchased twigs are generally stronger than those found in nature because they have been treated. Depending on the end-use for this project, you may opt to use the stronger type.

8.   Using small pieces of modeling compound, shape mittens and shoes. Push mittens and shoes onto twigs, then carefully remove. Place a drop of craft glue in each hole, then adhere twigs. Wipe away excess glue. Let dry.

9.   Using a dry paintbrush, dust inside of push mold with cornstarch.

10.   Pinch off pea-sized pieces of modeling compound, roll into a ball, and press into face push mold. Add more modeling compound to back of face to form the head. Release mold.

11.   Push molded head onto remaining twig, then carefully remove. Place a drop of craft glue in the hole, then adhere twig. Wipe away excess glue. Let dry.

12.   Using the paintbrush, apply a coat of découpage medium to the head, mittens, and shoes. Let dry.

13.   Paint head, mittens, and shoes with deep reddish brown paint. Allow to dry.

14.   Apply gold and copper leaf to head, mittens, and shoes by brushing a drop of découpage medium to painted areas, then pressing a small piece of gold or copper leaf into wet medium. Continue until shape is covered. Make certain some painted background shows through. Let dry. Apply a coat of découpage medium to gold and copper leaf. Let dry.

15.   Lay back leaf, wrong side up, on a flat surface. Determine placement of arms and legs. Place a piece of polyester stuffing at center of leaf. Lay twigs in their appropriate positions on top of the polyester stuffing.

16.   Squeeze a bead of hot glue across the twigs and the polyester stuffing. Using a spoon, place another piece of polyester stuffing onto the hot glue.

17.   Apply a fine bead of craft glue along the outside edges of the back leaf. Place leaf shapes together, matching edges as closely as possible. Press and hold until bond is secure.

18.   To tuck excess polyester stuffing inside leaf, lift edge while glue is still wet. Using a bamboo skewer, push polyester stuffing inside and reseal the opening. Let dry.

19.   To make the hair, adhere a small piece of reindeer moss to top of head with hot glue.

shining bright

List of supplies:

- Acrylic paint, metallic gold

- Card stock, yellow, 8¹/₂" x 11" sheet

- Chalk, flesh

- Cosmetic tissue

- Craft glue

- Craft knife, sharp

- Découpage medium, satin finish

- Embossing powder, yellow

- Embossing powder, extra-thick, clear

- Foam-core board, white, 5" x 10"

- Heat gun

- Masking tape

- Paintbrush, ¹/₂" flat

- Paper, 8¹/₂" x 11": dark brown, assorted shades of yellow

(Continued on page 64)

sunflower gal

(Continued from page 63)

- Paper punches: various flowers, extra-small sun

- Pigment ink stamp pad, yellow

- Scissors, sharp

- Spray glitter, ultrafine, gold

- Stylus

- Wrapping tissue, patterned

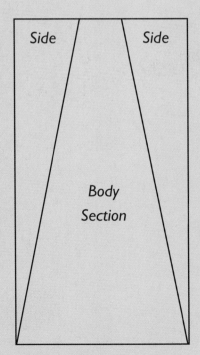

Diagram A

Instructions:

1. Make a black-and-white photocopy, enlarged to 200%, of the Body Pattern on page 65. Make a black-and-white photocopy of the Sunflower and Face Patterns on page 65. Using scissors, cut out body, sunflower, and face.

2. Place Body Pattern at center of foam-core board as shown in Diagram A at left and secure with masking tape.

3. Using a craft knife, cut body from foam-core board leaving a triangle at each side, as shown in Diagram A at left. Remove the body pattern.

4. Place the two triangular-shaped sides, wide side down, to form a standing body. Mark all upward facing surfaces.

5. Place a sheet of wrapping tissue face down on a flat surface. Arrange the body and the sides, marked-sides down, onto the wrapping tissue.

6. Using scissors, cut the wrapping tissue around the foam-core board pieces leaving a 1" margin on all sides. Set each piece of foam-core board and corresponding wrapping tissue aside.

7. Beginning with the largest piece, lay wrapping tissue face down on surface. Using a paintbrush, apply a coat of découpage medium to upper surface of foam-core board. Place on wrapping tissue to adhere. Glue over edges to the back side. Smooth wrapping tissue with fingers. Trim excess wrapping tissue as necessary. Let dry.

8. Repeat Step 7 above for remaining pieces of foam-core board.

9. Repeat Step 7 above to cover the remaining areas on the back side of foam-core board pieces with wrapping tissue scraps. Let dry.

10. Place Sunflower Pattern on yellow card stock and trace. Cut out.

11. Using a pigment stamp pad, apply ink to the front surface of the sunflower. Apply a generous layer of yellow embossing powder. Tap off excess. Using a heat gun, emboss sunflower.

12. Apply clear extra-thick embossing powder. Emboss, then set aside to cool.

13. Using craft glue, adhere Face Pattern to yellow card stock.

14. Using cosmetic tissue, apply a layer of chalk over face. Rub well to blend and work into surface of paper. Using a red pencil, blush cheeks and lips.

15. Adhere face to back side of embossed sunflower petals.

16. Attach triangular-shaped sides to center piece of covered foam-core board.

17. Using découpage medium, attach sunflower to top of figure.

Hint: Découpage medium seems to make paper curl and wrinkle less than craft glue. It also remains more flexible over time.

18. Using paper punches, punch flower shapes from a variety of yellow-colored papers. Punch flower centers from dark brown paper. Glue flower shapes together to "double," then add centers to each one.

19. Attach flowers to figure.

20. Using a stylus, randomly add dots with metallic gold acrylic paint.

21. Spray with two light coats of glitter spray. Let dry between each coat.

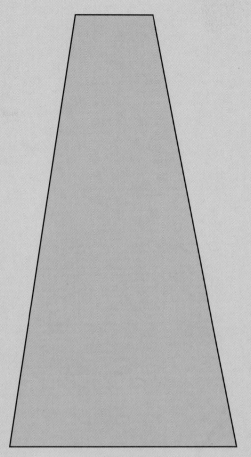

Body Pattern

Sunflower Pattern

Face Pattern

bangled harem doll

- Acrylic paints: pale metallic gold, dark green pearl
- Beading wire, metallic gold
- Brass bells (5)
- Craft glue
- Craft wire, 18-gauge
- Decorative yarn
- Découpage medium, satin finish
- Glitter spray, ultrafine, gold
- Hand-sewing needle
- Japanese paper, fibrous, heavy-weight
- Nonwrinkling paper glue
- Paintbrushes: 1" China-bristle, #6 round, stiff-bristle
- Paper towels
- Paper-twist ribbon, pale pink

(Continued on page 67)

Instructions:

1. Using a stiff-bristle paintbrush, gently brush twigs to remove dust and any loose matter.

2. Dampen a paper towel with rubbing alcohol and wipe twigs.

3. Using a #6 round paintbrush, apply a coat of découpage medium to twigs. Let dry.

4. Tear patterned wrapping tissue into $1/4$" x 8" strips.

5. Apply découpage medium to wrong side of first wrapping tissue strip. Beginning at tip of twig, wrap with wrapping tissue, covering tip and working toward the opposite end.

6. Repeat Step 5 above until all three twigs are completely covered with two layers of wrapping tissue. Let dry.

7. Seal with a coat of découpage medium.

8. Using scissors, cut one 7" x 20" piece from patterned wrapping tissue and one 7" x 20" piece from white wrapping tissue.

9. To crimp each piece of wrapping tissue, lightly roll it around a wooden dowel. Hold the dowel perpendicular to the table and firmly push the wrapping tissue downward. Remove and smooth. Repeat, working from top to bottom and from side to side. Roll and crimp edges and shape with fingers.

10. Using a 1" China-bristle paintbrush, apply nonwrinkling paper glue to one side of the white wrapping tissue. Adhere to wrong side of the patterned wrapping tissue. Let dry.

Hint: This makes a "lining" and strengthens the wrapping tissue.

11. To crimp the double-sided wrapping tissue, repeat Step 9 above.

12. Fold wrapping tissue, patterned sides out, to make a $3 1/2$" x 20" rectangle.

13. Using a hand-sewing needle and a doubled length of thread, make small running stitches at the top of rectangle. Tightly gather to $3 1/2$". Tie off.

14. Lay gathered wrapping tissue on a flat surface. Lay one prepared twig at outside edge at each end. Position top of twig at gathering line and bottom of twig extending below "cuff line" of pantaloons.

(Continued from page 66)

- Pigment ink, light green
- Polyester stuffing
- Rubber stamp, long leaf
- Rubbing alcohol
- Scissors, sharp
- String
- Thread
- Toothpick
- Transparent tape
- Twigs, approximately $1/4$"-diameter x $3 1/2$"-long
- Wire cutters
- Wooden dowel, $3/8$"-diameter
- Wrapping tissues: patterned, white

15. Using the #6 round paintbrush, apply découpage medium to the twig, covering area from the top to $^1/_2$" from the bottom. To make the pantaloons, roll the twig and the wrapping tissue toward the center. Repeat steps for the remaining leg.

16. Tie with string at waistline and at cuff line to secure while drying. Let dry for one hour.

17. Cut one $2^1/_2$"-square paper-twist ribbon. To crimp the ribbon, repeat Step 9 on page 67.

18. Place a walnut-sized tuft of polyester stuffing in center of square. Hold tip of remaining prepared twig to center of paper and stuffing. Wrap end of twig as if wrapping a lollipop. Wrap craft wire around the neck to secure the paper to the twig.

19. Using a long-leaf-shaped rubber stamp and light green pigment ink, stamp two leaves onto Japanese paper.

20. Using the #6 round paintbrush, paint the stamped side of leaves with pale metallic gold. Let dry. Add details with dark green pearl. Let dry. Cut out.

Hint: If desired, additional layers of color can be added.

21. Using wire cutters, cut two lengths from craft wire measuring 1" longer than stamped leaves. Cut two lengths from transparent tape the same length as the wires. Place each piece of wire to the center of tape. Turn leaf cutouts upside down and run the wires from the tips to the ends. Smooth tape to seal.

22. Apply one coat of découpage medium to the back side of each leaf. Press onto Japanese paper so the wire and tape are between the layers. Let dry. Cut out.

23. Stipple-paint the unpainted side of each leaf with pale metallic gold and dark green pearl. Let dry.

24. To attach the leaf arms, point each leaf upward at the shoulders. Glue arms to twig with craft glue. Let dry. Wrap beading wire around the glued area to secure arms.

25. To attach the torso to the pantaloons, glue bottom of twig in the waistline opening as shown in Diagram A at right. Using a toothpick, spread a thin layer of craft glue inside gathers. Wrap gathers around the twig and squeeze together. Wrap craft wire around the waistline to secure paper to twig.

26. Cut a 1½" equilateral triangle from Japanese paper. Stipple-paint with pale metallic gold and dark green pearl. Let dry.

27. To make the bodice, glue triangle to front of figure. Let dry. Trim excess at back as necessary. Glue loose edges. Let dry.

28. Tightly wrap decorative yarn around wire at neck and waistline and around string at cuff lines. Secure ends with a drop of craft glue.

29. Using wire cutters, cut beading wire into four 6" lengths. Slide one brass bell to center of each length of wire. Twist to secure. Position one bell around neck and twist wire over yarn. Repeat at waistline and at cuff lines.

30. To make the turban, cut one 1½" x 5" piece from patterned wrapping tissue. To crimp wrapping tissue, repeat Step 9 on page 67.

31. Fold wrapping tissue, patterned sides out, to make a ¾" x 5" rectangle.

32. Using the hand-sewing needle and a doubled length of thread, make small running stitches at the top of rectangle. Tightly gather and tie off.

33. Glue gathered edge around head. Let dry. Shape into a turban and glue a bell to top.

34. Spray with two light coats of glitter spray. Let dry between each coat. Position arms as desired. Spray tops of arms with a light coat of glitter spray. Let dry.

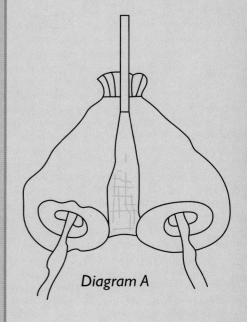

Diagram A

Design tip:

Hands and shoes can easily be added to this figure. Follow the instructions for the "Leaf Man," Step 8, on page 62.

List of supplies for one muse:

- Acrylic varnish, satin finish
- Cardboard, lightweight
- Cornstarch
- Creative Paperclay® modeling compound, white, 3 oz.
- Découpage medium, satin finish
- Gesso, white
- Hot-glue gun and glue sticks
- Masking tape
- Paintbrush, $^1/_2$" flat
- Paper, $8^1/_2$" x 11", 2 sheets
- Paper towel tube
- Push mold, face
- Scissors, sharp
- Wooden pencil
- Wrapping tissue, white

the muses

Instructions:

1. Using a dry paintbrush, dust inside of push mold with cornstarch.

2. Pinch off one walnut-sized piece of modeling compound, roll it into a ball, and press into push mold. Release mold. Let set for approximately 15 minutes.

3. Position molded face on tube and gently work shape to fit curvature. Remove and let dry.

4. Using a pencil, trace around bottom of tube onto lightweight cardboard. Using scissors, cut shape from cardboard. Fit into bottom of tube and secure with masking tape.

5. Randomly tear paper into 1" x 11" strips. Using the paintbrush, apply paper strips to tube, including bottom of tube, with découpage medium. Let dry. Repeat with two additional layers.

6. Apply a thin layer of découpage medium to back side of the molded face. Attach molded face to tube. Let dry.

7. Roll modeling compound into $^{1}/_{4}$" coil. To make the hood, shape around face and smooth outside seams.

8. To make the breasts, pinch off two small pieces of modeling compound. Shape and attach with découpage medium. Let dry.

9. Seal entire figure with two light coats of découpage medium. Let dry between each coat.

10. Draw vertical lines from top of tube to within 1" from bottom of tube with hot glue. Remove stray "strings" and/or "droplets" of glue.

Hint: Avoid placing hot-glue lines over face.

11. Using the paintbrush, apply two coats of gesso to entire figure. Let dry between each coat.

12. Randomly tear wrapping tissue into strips and squares. Using the paintbrush, apply wrapping tissue pieces to tube, except face area, with découpage medium. Let dry. Repeat with two additional layers.

Hint: Use the paintbrush to push wrapping tissue pieces into recessed areas and to smooth and blend seams.

13. Repeat Step 11 above.

14. Using the paintbrush, apply two light coats of acrylic varnish to entire figure. Let dry between each coat.

Design tips:

Make three individual figures and tie them together with decorative cord. Wire and beads can be used to add a contemporary flair to this project.

To use as a candleholder, you can fill figure $^{3}/_{4}$ full with dry rice, beans, or decorative gravel. Position candle, then figure can be stuffed to the top with decorative tissue or cellophane.

in the spotlight

silhouettes

List of supplies:

- Cuticle scissors, sharp
- Decorative paper
- Frame, narrow
- Masking tape
- Nonwrinkling paper glue
- Paintbrush, #6 round
- Paper, 20# text, black

Instructions:

1. Make a black-and-white photocopy, enlarged as desired, of the three Silhouette Patterns at right.

2. Adhere patterns to black paper with small pieces of masking tape.

3. Using scissors, cut out patterns and paper simultaneously. Carefully remove patterns and masking tape.

4. Using a paintbrush, apply nonwrinkling paper glue to back side of each silhouette. Adhere to decorative paper. Let dry.

Hint: Apply glue, beginning at center of cut-out figure, brushing glue toward outer edges.

5. Frame as desired.

Silhouette Patterns

List of supplies:

- Acrylic paints: bronze, dark green, medium green
- Acrylic varnish, satin finish
- Bamboo skewer
- Card stock, 8½" x 11"
- Cornstarch
- Corsage pin
- Craft knife
- Creative Paperclay® modeling compound, white, 6 oz.
- Decorative buttons, assorted shapes and sizes
- Découpage medium, satin finish
- Disposable cup
- Fabric, 6" square
- Glazing medium, clear
- Hand-sewing needle
- Hot-glue gun and glue sticks

(Continued on page 75)

pre–colombian jar man

Instructions:

1. Using scissors, cut two $2\frac{1}{2}$" squares from card stock. Roll card stock squares into cone shapes with $\frac{3}{4}$" openings at tops and $\frac{1}{2}$" openings at bottoms. Secure with masking tape.

2. Cut four $\frac{1}{2}$" x 10" strips from wrapping tissue. Using a paintbrush, apply a coat of découpage medium to the strips of wrapping tissue. Wrap each cone with two strips of wrapping tissue. Let dry.

3. Cut both cones in half as shown in Diagram A on page 76. Set the pieces with the $\frac{1}{2}$" diameter openings aside.

4. Apply découpage medium to the insides of the remaining halves. Firmly stuff each half with small pieces of wrapping tissue leaving a small space at the narrow end of each cone.

5. Push one wooden bead into each narrow end as shown in Diagram B on page 76 and adhere in place with hot glue. Let dry.

6. Repeat Step 4 above for the previously set-aside halves.

7. To make each leg, bent at the knee, push part of the exposed portion of each wooden bead into the narrow end of each cone as shown in Diagram C on page 76 and adhere in place with hot glue. Allow to dry.

8. Pinch off one walnut-sized piece of modeling compound, roll into a ball, and press into open end of cone at ankle. Shape into a boot. Repeat for remaining leg.

9. Cut two $\frac{1}{2}$" x 10" strips from wrapping tissue. Using a paintbrush, apply a coat of découpage medium to the strips of wrapping tissue. Wrap area around each wooden ball (knee) with one strip of wrapping tissue. Let dry.

10. Using a pencil, mark line on papier-mâché box around bottom edge of lid. Remove lid and set aside.

11. Position legs on box as desired and mark placement.

12. Using the paintbrush, apply two coats of découpage medium to inside and outside surfaces of papier-mâché box and lid. Let dry.

13. To make the embossed designs, begin by making the molds. To do this, pinch off several walnut-sized pieces of polymer clay, roll into balls, and slightly press to flatten until they are approximately $\frac{1}{4}$" thick. Using a dry paintbrush, dust decorative part of buttons and tops

(Continued from page 74)

- Masking tape
- Needle-nosed pliers
- Paintbrush, #6 round
- Paper towels
- Papier-mâché box with lid, 3"-diameter
- Polyester stuffing
- Polymer clay
- Push mold, face
- Scissors, sharp
- Thread
- Wire cutters
- Wooden beads, $\frac{1}{2}$" (2)
- Wooden candle cup, 2"
- Wooden pencil
- Wrapping tissue, white

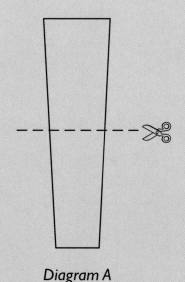

Diagram A

Diagram B

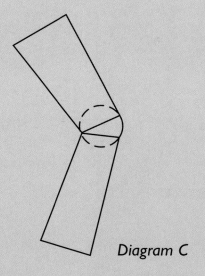

Diagram C

of clay with cornstarch. Press the buttons into the clay, then carefully remove. Bake the molds according to manufacturer's instructions. Let cool.

14.   Dust inside of molds with cornstarch.

15.   Pinch off pea-sized pieces of modeling compound, roll into balls, and press into molds. Set aside two symmetrical pieces to be used as earrings.

16.   Apply découpage medium to the backs of the embossed designs. Carefully place on legs, beginning with the largest pieces. Hold in place until secure, adding additional découpage medium as needed. Continue covering surfaces of legs with varying shapes and sizes, stopping approximately 1" from tops of leg. Let dry.

Hint: Some "gaps" will appear because of the irregularity of shapes and sizes. To fill in these areas, roll tiny balls of modeling compound and press into open spaces. Gently press the center of each ball with the flat end of a bamboo skewer.

17.   Adhere legs to box with hot glue.

18.   Continue adding embossed designs around box, up to pencil line where lid will fit, as in Step 16 above.

19.   Seal embossed designs with two coats of découpage medium. Let dry.

20.   Apply two coats of découpage medium to inside and outside of wooden candle cup. Let dry.

21.   Using a dry paintbrush, dust inside of face push mold with cornstarch.

22.   Pinch off pea-sized pieces of modeling compound, roll into a ball, and press into push mold. Release mold. Let set for approximately 30 minutes.

23.   Using a craft knife, carefully trim excess modeling compound from back of molded face until it is approximately $1/2$" thick.

24.   Determine face placement on candle cup. Using the paintbrush, apply a thin layer of découpage medium to the candle cup where the face will be placed and to the back of the molded face. Attach molded face, blending edges with the paintbrush dampened with water. Let dry.

25. To make the ears, roll modeling compound into ¹/₂"-long coils. Shape the ears as desired and attach as in Step 24 on page 76. Let dry for 24 hours.

26. Adhere head to top center of box lid with hot glue.

27. Cover top and sides of lid with embossed designs as in Step 16 on page 76.

28. To make the hat, cut one 4"-diameter circle from fabric. Using a hand-sewing needle and a doubled length of thread, make small running stitches at outside edge of fabric circle. Gather and loosely fill with polyester stuffing. Tightly pull and tie off. Place inside candle cup opening and adhere in place with hot glue.

29. Place a corsage pin down through center of hat. Using needle-nosed pliers, work the corsage pin through hole in bottom of candle cup and into box lid. If necessary, clip sharp point on inside of box lid with wire cutters.

30. Using the paintbrush, paint entire figure inside and outside with two coats of medium green paint. Let dry between each coat.

31. Mix three drops of dark green paint and three drops of glazing medium in a disposable cup. Using the paintbrush, paint entire figure, working into recessed areas. Using a paper towel, wipe paint/glazing medium mixture from raised surface areas. Let dry.

32. Using your finger, apply bronze paint onto raised surface areas of box and lid. Build depth of color as desired.

33. Using the paintbrush, apply two light coats of acrylic varnish to entire figure. Let dry between each coat.

patchwork pauper

List of supplies:

- Acrylic paints: black, flesh, pink, white
- Brass charm
- Card stock, heavy, 11" x 14"
- Cellulose powder
- Cornstarch
- Craft glue
- Craft knife, sharp
- Creative Paperclay® modeling compound, white, 3 oz.
- Decorative trim, braid, $^1/_4$ yard
- Découpage medium, satin finish
- Double jump ring
- Fabric, 1" square (2)
- Greeting cards
- Hair, curly wool
- Hot-glue gun and glue sticks
- Measuring spoons
- Miniature broom
- Mixing bowl, large
- Paintbrush, #6 round
- Paper towels
- Plastic dishpan, 12-quart

(Continued on page 79)

Instructions:

1. Using a dry paintbrush, dust inside of push mold with cornstarch.

2. Pinch off pea-sized pieces of modeling compound, roll into a ball, and press into push mold. Release the mold. Let set for approximately 30 minutes.

3. Using a craft knife, carefully trim excess modeling compound from back of molded face until it is approximately $1/2$" thick.

4. Roll card stock into cone shape. Secure at seam line with transparent tape.

5. Using scissors, trim around bottom edge of cone to adjust height.

6. Make the papier-mâché pulp as with Pinecone Santa, Steps 1–4, on page 17.

7. Place a paper towel flat on a rigid surface. Place a walnut-sized piece of papier-mâché on the paper towel and flatten until it is approximately $1/4$" thick. Remove papier-mâché from the paper towel and wrap around the cone. Smooth with fingers, smoothing and blending as necessary. Let dry for 24 hours.

Hint: If too much moisture or weight is added to the cone too quickly, it will collapse.

8. Make the sleeves from papier-mâché and attach to robe.

9. Using the paintbrush, apply a thin layer of découpage medium to the top of the cone where the face will be placed and to the back of the molded face. Attach molded face, blending edges with the paintbrush dampened with water. Let dry.

10. Using the paintbrush, paint face with flesh, eyes with black, eyebrows with white, and cheeks and lips with pink. Let dry.

11. Cut old greeting cards into triangular- and rectangular-shaped pieces. Glue pieces, overlapping as necessary, to entire figure with craft glue. Seal entire figure with two light coats of découpage medium. Let dry between each coat.

12. To make the mittens, wrap small pieces of polyester stuffing with fabric. Tightly tie around the tops with thread.

13. Place mittens in sleeves and attach with hot glue. Glue hair on head. To make the earring, glue double jump ring to one side of face. Glue decorative trim around collar, sleeves, and hemline. Glue brass charm to collar. Glue broom between mittens.

(Continued from page 78)

- Polyester stuffing
- Push mold, face
- Scissors, sharp
- Sieve, fine
- Table fork
- Thread
- Toilet paper, 2-ply, 1 roll
- Transparent tape
- Wire whisk

Design tip:

If using heavy-weight cards, pieces must be cut very small in order to cover rounded areas. This process will give a mosaic effect to the figure's surface. Christmas wrapping paper, cut or torn, also works well.

the season's best

greeting card holder

List of supplies:

- Acrylic paints: coordinating colors
- Acrylic varnish spray, satin finish
- Adhesive sealant
- Craft knife
- Découpage medium, satin finish
- Embellishments, as desired
- Gesso, white
- Greeting cards (2)
- Hot-glue gun and glue sticks
- Natural sponge
- Paintbrush, $1/2$" flat
- Plywood: 12" x 12" x $1/4$"; $1^3/4$" x $5^1/4$" x $1/2$"
- Router
- Scroll saw
- Wood clamps
- Wooden base, 6" x 3" x $3/4$"
- Wooden pencil

Instructions:

1.   Using a craft knife, cut artwork from greeting cards for front and back of card holder.

2.   Using a pencil, trace perimeter of artwork onto $1/4$"-thick plywood.

3.   Using a scroll saw, cut front and back of card holder from the plywood pieces.

4.   Using a router, miter sides of wooden base at a 70° angle.

5.   Using a paintbrush, apply gesso to plywood pieces. Let dry.

6.   Using a natural sponge, sponge-paint plywood pieces and wooden base with coordinating colors of acrylic paints.

7.   Using the paintbrush, apply a thin layer of découpage medium to back sides of the cut-out artwork and adhere to the corresponding plywood pieces in perfect alignment. Apply découpage medium over top of artwork. Let dry.

8.   Embellish artwork as desired.

9.   Adhere front and back of card holder onto $1/2$"-thick plywood support with adhesive sealant. Using wood clamps, clamp into position and let dry. Adhere support to base. Let dry.

10.   Spray with two light coats of acrylic varnish. Let dry between each coat.

Design tip:

Synthetic "snow-in-a-jar" used in decorative painting adds texture and depth to this type of project. Make certain to follow the manufacturer's instructions.

stylish profile

the mannequin

Instructions:

1. Using a fine-blade saw, cut 3" off top of wooden spindle. Wipe away excess dust.

2. To make the finial, attach wooden ball to top of 3" length of spindle with craft glue. Let dry.

3. Using an electric drill with $1/16$" drill bit, drill a hole through bottom center of wooden bowl and up through bottom of 11" length of spindle. To make the base, screw spindle to wooden bowl.

4. Using a $1/2$" flat paintbrush, apply a generous coat of découpage medium to all wooden pieces and to papier-mâché torso. Let dry.

5. Using the paintbrush, apply gesso to all wooden pieces and to papier-mâché torso. Let dry.

6. Pour one teaspoon each of light ivory, dark ivory, and light tan paints and two teaspoons glazing medium into separate puddles on a disposable plate. Using a #6 stipple paintbrush, stipple-paint finial and base using deeper colors at the bottom and working into lighter colors at the top.

Hint: Using glazing medium with each color as it is applied will make blending easier.

7. Randomly stipple-paint finial and base with pale metallic gold paint and glazing medium. Let dry.

8. Using the $1/2$" flat paintbrush, paint areas at tops of shoulders, across abdomen, and down hip areas at front of torso with dark metallic bronze paint. Paint areas under shoulders and across buttocks at back of torso. Let dry.

9. Apply a light coat of crackle medium to dark metallic bronze-painted areas. Let dry. Brush over surface with light ivory paint until torso has crackled surface.

10. Repeat Steps 6–7 above over uncracked areas.

11. Attach finial and base to torso with craft glue. Let dry.

12. Spray with three light coats of acrylic varnish. Let dry between each coat.

List of supplies:

- Acrylic paints: dark bronze, dark ivory, light ivory, pale metallic gold, light tan
- Acrylic varnish spray, satin finish
- Crackle medium
- Craft glue
- Découpage medium, matte finish
- Disposable plate
- Electric drill with $1/16$" drill bit
- Gesso, white
- Glazing medium, clear
- Paintbrushes: $1/2$" flat, #6 stipple
- Papier-mâché torso
- Saw, fine-blade
- Screwdriver
- Wood screw, $2 1/4$"
- Wooden ball, $1 1/2$"-diameter
- Wooden bowl, 6"-diameter
- Wooden spindle, 14"

in good form

stamped silhouette

List of supplies:

- Acrylic paints: lavender, metallic gold, pale yellow green
- Craft knife, sharp
- Cutting mat
- Disposable plate
- Envelope, 9" x 12"
- Masking tape
- Measuring spoons
- Pigment ink, black
- Rubber stamps: small butterfly, various-sized and styled designs
- Synthetic sponge
- Transparency plastic, 8 1/2" x 11" sheet

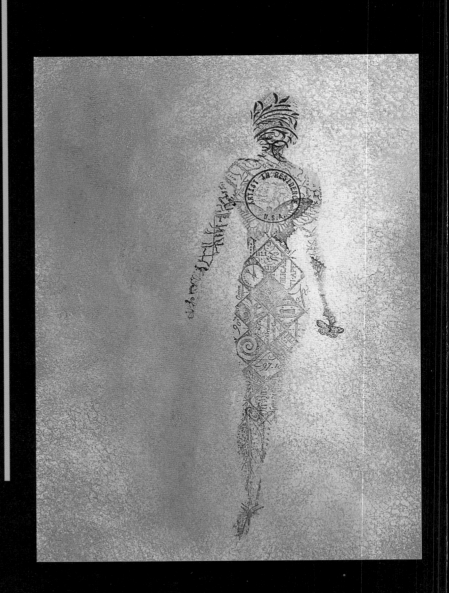

Instructions:

1. Make a black-and-white photocopy, at 100%, of the Walking Figure Pattern at right.

2. Place enlarged pattern under transparency plastic and secure with masking tape at edges. Place on cutting mat.

3. Using a craft knife, cut out figure and create a stencil. Remove and discard masking tape and pattern. Set figure and stencil aside.

4. Pour $^1/_2$ teaspoon each of lavender, pale yellow green, and metallic gold paints into separate puddles on a disposable plate.

5. Using a synthetic sponge, sponge-paint left side and bottom of envelope with lavender. Let dry. Repeat sponge-painting, working toward center, with pale yellow green. Let dry. Continue with metallic gold. Let dry.

6. Place stencil at center of sponged envelope and secure with masking tape. Heavily sponge-paint stencil opening (figure) with metallic gold. With stencil in place, let dry.

7. Using rubber stamps, randomly stamp various designs on figure with black pigment ink. Let dry. Carefully remove masking tape and the stencil.

8. Using a small butterfly rubber stamp, stamp a single butterfly in one of the figure's hands. Allow to dry.

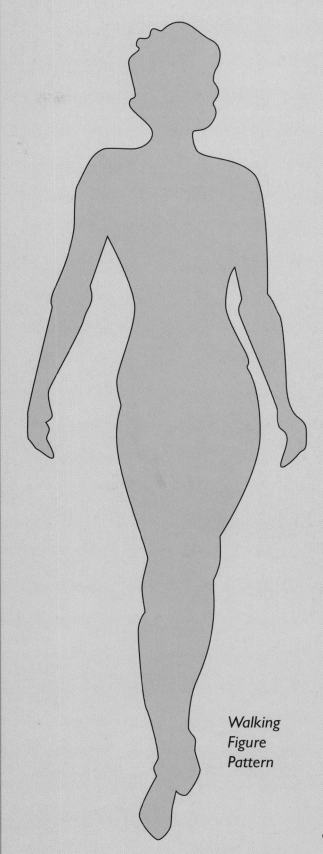

Walking Figure Pattern

masquerade

**List of supplies
for one marionette:**

- Art board
- Card stock, heavy
- Embroidery floss
  or ribbon
- Embroidery needle
- Grommets or brads
- Scissors, sharp
- Spray mount

Designed by:
Caroll Shreeve

These marionettes
were inspired by
authentic antique
playing cards.
Use as they are
here for decorative
wall plaques or
create workable
marionettes.

Instructions:

1. Make a photocopy from the artwork provided on pages 88 and 89 onto card stock.

Hint: Coloring books, clip art, or personal drawings also can be used.

2. Spray-mount each marionette onto art board.

3. Using scissors, carefully cut out marionette.

4. At hinge points, puncture with needle and embroidery floss. Use all six strands.

5. Knot embroidery floss or ribbon at hinge indicators at wrists, elbows, knees, and ankles, as desired.

Hint: A needle threader is helpful to pull ribbon through hinge points.

6. A decorated piece of card stock can serve as a puppeteer's operating device. Pierce holes and pull floss through, knotting at back.

Hint: If you want your marionettes to really work, make each limb separate and attach at the joints with grommets or brads.

Design tip:

Color-photocopy the marionettes and their string holders onto card stock or pressure-sensitive clear label film. Card stock dolls make effective wall hangings. Having been inspired by playing cards, they would be interesting conversation pieces in a room where card games are played. Dolls on clear film can be transparent window art.

lovely in linen

hanky doll

Designed by:
Caroll Shreeve

List of supplies for one doll:

- Card stock, heavy
- Craft knife, sharp
- Dressmaker's glass-head pin or hat pin with bead or pearl head
- Foam-core board, white, 5" x 10"
- Handkerchief, lace-edged
- Iron
- Scissors, sharp
- Spray mount

Instructions:

1. Make a photocopy from the artwork provided at right onto card stock.

2. Spray-mount doll onto foam-core board. Using a craft knife, cut out doll, allowing for a stand at the feet.

Hint: A simple slit in the base between the feet can be fitted with another scrap of foam-core board to make the doll stand.

3. Press handkerchief and fold it around doll with its edges forming a point at the corner, triangular-style.

4. Securely pin handkerchief at back of doll so pin point is hidden in folds of handkerchief.

If you should shed a tear

or feel the need to sneeze

Just use this pretty hanky

if you care to please.

Gift idea:

Purchase a beautiful lace-edged handkerchief or personally crochet the edges of one. Tuck it around this paper doll or one of your own. A translucent vellum gift envelope is ideal for the presentation of your gift.

classic style

List of supplies:

- *Copy paper, lightweight*
- *Craft knife, sharp*
- *Foam-core board, white, 4" x 8"*
- *Scissors, sharp*
- *Spray mount*

Designed by:
Caroll Shreeve

Design tip:

Using a light-table, create more outfits for your doll by lightly taping the doll to the glass, covering her with a fresh sheet of copy paper, and designing your own gowns. Color them, cut them out, and add them to her trousseau.

Instructions:

1. Make a color photocopy from the doll artwork provided on page 92 onto copy paper. Enlarge or reduce as desired.

Hint: Larger dolls and clothing require less dexterity to cut and manipulate with tabs.

2. Spray-mount doll onto foam-core board. Using a craft knife, cut out allowing for a stand at the feet.

Hint: A simple slit in the base between the feet can be fitted with another scrap of foam-core board to make the doll stand.

3. Make a color photocopy from the clothes artwork provided on pages 93–94 and at right onto copy paper.

Hint: If embellishments are desired, you may choose to photocopy artwork onto card stock.

4. Using scissors, cut out clothes, making certain to carefully cut out tabs. Fold tabs along dotted lines and enjoy mixing and matching the doll's outfits.

95

List of supplies:

- Acrylic paints, assorted colors
- Acrylic varnish, satin finish
- Beads
- Craft glue
- Craft knife, sharp
- Fibers
- Foam-core board, white
- Masking tape
- Mini cutters
- Needle-nosed pliers
- Paintbrush, $^1/_2$" flat
- Paper, $8^1/_2$" x 11": assorted decorative and textured sheets
- Polymer clay or Creative Paperclay® modeling compound
- Rubber stamps, various-sized and styled designs
- Scissors, sharp
- Tweezers
- Wire
- Wire cutters

Designed by: Diana Twedt

a glimpse from the past

petroglyphic profile

Instructions:

1. Make a black-and-white photocopy of the Body Pattern at right. Using scissors, cut out body.

2. Place Body Pattern at center of foam-core board and secure with masking tape.

3. Using a craft knife, cut body from foam-core board. Remove the pattern.

4. Adhere papers to body in a collage fashion with craft glue.

Hint: Layering torn papers creates an interesting surface on the body of the figure.

5. Using a paintbrush, apply two light coats of acrylic varnish to seal papers. Let dry between each coat.

6. Form a face for the figure from polymer clay or modeling compound. Roll out clay and impress with rubber stamps or create shapes with mini cutters. Bake the clay according to manufacturer's instructions. Let cool. Paint with acrylic paints.

7. Adhere to figure. Accent by dry-brushing details with acrylic paints.

8. Embellish figure with wire, beads, and/or fibers as desired.

9. Attach a hanging device to back of figure.

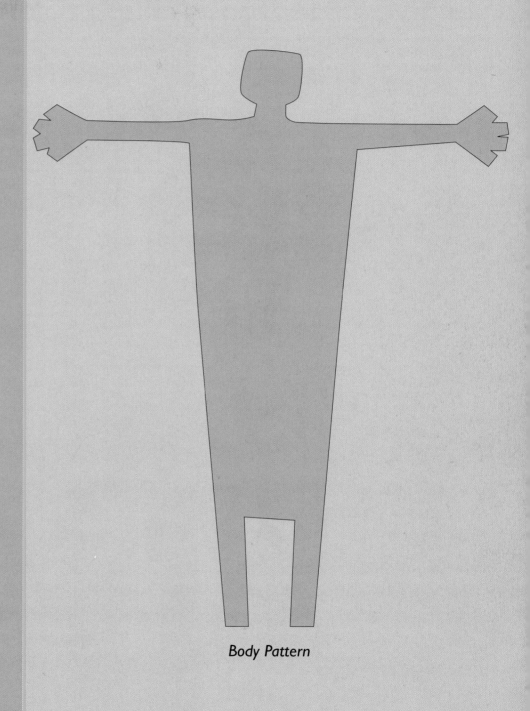

Body Pattern

Gallery of Dolls

Diana Twedt

Diana Twedt

Allen & Patty Eckman

Jacques Dorier   Photo by George Post

Toni Carroll   Photo by Don Smith

Jacques Dorier   Photo by George Post

diana twedt

Twedt of Rudyard, Montana, has worked primarily with batik for the past 20 years. More recently she has been creating mixed-media collages that combine paper batik, handmade papers, paper clay, and found objects that express her interest in color and texture.

A graduate of Montana State University-Bozeman, Twedt earned a B.A. in Art Education and recently concluded 15 years in public schools teaching visual arts to kindergarten through twelfth grade students. She now devotes her energy to personal artistic growth and works with paper in a wide range of applications, from jewelry and collages to embellishing furniture.

Twedt is inspired by her experiences as a teacher and credits her students with helping her appreciate the serendipity of art-making and the joy of creating. "Art is a hopeful process," Twedt states. "There is so much optimism involved in creating from simple materials that hold infinite possibilities."

The peace and freedom of rural life has been the perfect setting for Twedt's creative endeavors. She resides on the family farm with her husband Russ and two grown children. Twedt exhibits her work with art associations in the area and in several Montana galleries, and is a contributor to Somerset Studio magazine.

pattie bibb

Throughout her life, Bibb has enjoyed an avid interest in creating with her hands. Summer craft courses and art classes helped her develop expertise in several media.

Some small black-cloth dolls in a magazine inspired her first doll "without a face or shoulders." Bibb believes first dolls help reveal potential. New doll makers are often intimidated, and seeing the "first" doll of an experienced artist encourages others that they too can do it.

In 1992, Bibb was fortunate to take a class from NIADA artist, Robert McKinley. She was inspired by his wit and style and it was there she was introduced to paper clay. She immediately began combining paper clay with her first love—cloth. This combination enabled her to make three-dimensional painted cloth dolls.

Since 1998, Bibb has been teaching her unique method of paper clay over cloth to doll clubs and at national cloth doll seminars.

TREACLE
Patte Bibb

allen & patty eckman

Allen Eckman was born in South Gate, California, in 1946. From age 5 to 15, his parents, three brothers, and two sisters lived on a small farm in Pennsylvania. After returning to California, Eckman graduated from high school in 1965, then enlisted in the Marine Corps. Four years later, a Sgt. E-5 and decorated combat veteran of the Vietnam War, Eckman studied art. His formal education was completed at Art Center College of Design in 1974.

Patty Tenneboe-Eckman was born in Brookings, South Dakota, in 1950. She grew up in Rapid City and in 1965, her parents, two brothers, and one sister moved to the San Fernando Valley in Southern California. Tenneboe-Eckman's formal education was also completed at Art Center College of Design in 1974 and it was there the two met.

After college, the couple married and operated a small advertising company in the LA area while raising three children. Twelve years later, after deciding they had had enough of the stressful life of advertising artists in Southern California, they set out on a whole new career path which opened up an exciting and different world for both of them—the fine art of cast-paper sculpture.

After recognizing the possibilities this medium had to offer, they began to experiment and today are the inventors of a special cast-paper sculpture process which is trademarked.

Eckman has great interest in the Native American Indian, while Tenneboe-Eckman's interest is in wildlife, birds, and flowers. Since the year 2000, she has also been sculpting beautiful Indian women and children. On large complicated and detailed works, the couple often works together and both sign the piece when completed.

Now residing in Rapid City, South Dakota, their home and studio is in the beautiful Black Hills. It is there they find inspiration. The wildlife, the history, the climate, and the spirituality of their lives provide them with an enormous amount of creativity.

jacques dorier

Photo by George Post

This amusing Frenchman became a circus clown after dropping out of dental school. After many years of performing, he studied with a Japanese Master the fascinating art of Washi doll making. These three-dimensional dolls were entirely made of paper.

Dorier's recent work combines figurative sculpting, resin casting, paper manipulation techniques, fine painting, and a fearless imagination. This unusual combination lends itself to the creation of intricate paper sculptures with rich textural qualities. His background as a circus performer is evident in his use of bright colors and his vivid, whimsical approach to each subject.

His paper sculptures portray whimsical characters, fanciful maidens, and fantasy characters, as well as hilarious frogs and snails! Whatever the subject matter, the sculptures convey motion and seem ready to jump off the shelf.

An avid collector summed it up . . . "Jacques' sculptures have an attitude!"

Dorier states that his goal as an artist is to create objects of everlasting beauty and comfort; objects that soothe the soul and act as a peaceful refuge from our hectic world.

Famous collectors of Dorier's work include actress Demi Moore and the White House.

Photo by George Post

kim deneris–brown

Deneris-Brown's figures are kindred to both commedia dell'arte and old European puppetry. Her work is intuitive and she strives to let the figures define themselves.

She works in paper clay and is pleased with its response to her doll making. She also finds working with textiles extremely pleasurable. Their textures, colors, and patterns mix together and create interesting combinations with the dolls.

Deneris-Brown explores antique and second-hand shops and finds many treasures for her dolls. They have been featured in many doll and art publications and she has won an award for her creativity and use of fabric and color.

"Through my dolls I try and connect with another element within me, and share this fun and fantasy with others."

toni carroll

Carroll, a native of Jackson, Mississippi, received her formal education in Fine Arts and Interior Design at the University of Mississippi in Oxford, and Richland College in Dallas. She now resides in Orlando, Florida.

Involved in art from childhood, Carroll won many awards, including the First Place Art Award from the Mississippi Art Association while still a high-school senior. After a lengthy and happy career as a professional Interior Designer, Carroll saw some reproduction dolls. A couple of years of making dolls from molds left the artist longing to

Photo by Don Smith

create her own from scratch. One-of-a-kind custom-sculpted dolls soon followed. This artist is now able to combine her love of sculpting and her skills as a seamstress to create these interesting and unusual art pieces. Her dolls have been acquired by collectors all over the world, as well as having been featured in national magazines and books.

In 1992, Carroll was one of the founders of the Original Doll Artists Association (ODAA) which was formed to nurture doll artists and create a place where they could share and teach each other. Many fine and accomplished doll artists have emerged from this group.

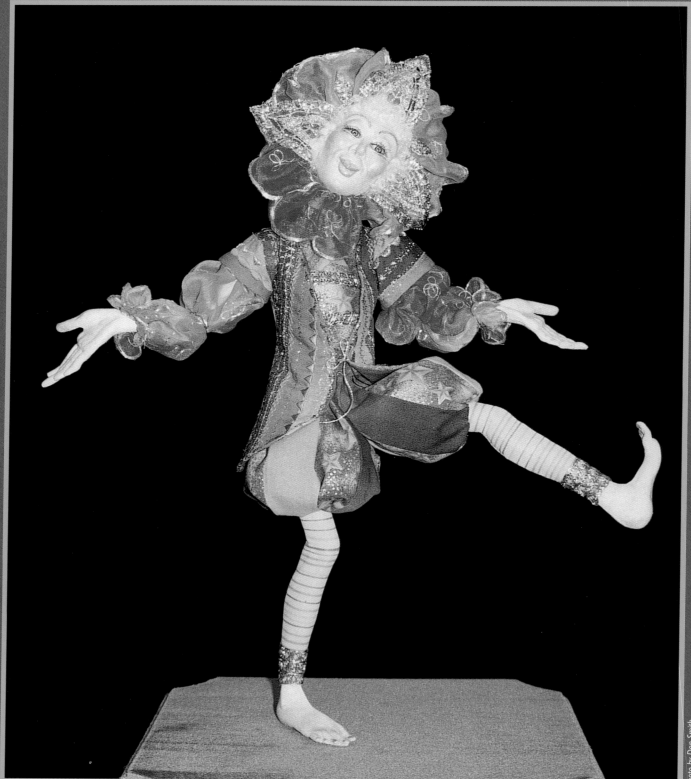

125

about the author

Dedication:

This book is dedicated to my angels—those seen and unseen.

Rhonda Rainey is an artist of many interests and talents. She is an award-winning watercolorist, designer, and published author. She has always loved drawing, painting, books, and dolls. She was blessed to grow up in a family who understood her interests and who encouraged her gifts and abilities.

Those associated with Rainey find her to be thoughtful and innovative when it comes to pushing the boundaries of established crafting techniques. She approaches each new project with a fresh and spirited perspective.

An art educator for more than 20 years, Rainey is currently working as a freelance artist and designer. Occasionally she returns to the classroom as a substitute teacher "to keep one foot" in the real world.

The mother of three grown children, and a fun-loving grandmother, she resides in Pocatello, Idaho.

Acknowledgments:

Heartfelt thanks to my family and friends for their love, support, encouragement, and patience.

My appreciation to editor, Cathy Sexton and art director Karla Haberstich, whose dedication, talent, and determination have made this book a reality.

Many thank-yous to the artists who contributed their exceptional work and shared their ideas in the gallery.

A special thank-you to Michael Gerbasi at Creative Paperclay® Company, Inc., for providing products used in this book and for answering technical questions.

metric conversions

INCHES TO MILLIMETRES AND CENTIMETRES

MM-Millimetres   CM-Centimetres

INCHES	MM	CM	INCHES	CM	INCHES	CM
$1/8$	3	0.9	9	22.9	30	76.2
$1/4$	6	0.6	10	25.4	31	78.7
$3/8$	10	1.0	11	27.9	32	81.3
$1/2$	13	1.3	12	30.5	33	83.8
$5/8$	16	1.6	13	33.0	34	86.4
$3/4$	19	1.9	14	35.6	35	88.9
$7/8$	22	2.2	15	38.1	36	91.4
1	25	2.5	16	40.6	37	94.0
$1\,1/4$	32	3.2	17	43.2	38	96.5
$1\,1/2$	38	3.8	18	45.7	39	99.1
$1\,3/4$	44	4.4	19	48.3	40	101.6
2	51	5.1	20	50.8	41	104.1
$2\,1/2$	64	6.4	21	53.3	42	106.7
3	76	7.6	22	55.9	43	109.2
$3\,1/2$	89	8.9	23	58.4	44	111.8
4	102	10.2	24	61.0	45	114.3
$4\,1/2$	114	11.4	25	63.5	46	116.8
5	127	12.7	26	66.0	47	119.4
6	152	15.2	27	68.6	48	121.9
7	178	17.8	28	71.1	49	124.5
8	203	20.3	29	73.7	50	127.0

YARDS TO METRES

YARDS	METRES	YARDS	METRES	YARDS	METRES	YARDS	METRES	YARDS	METRES
$1/8$	0.11	$2\,1/8$	1.94	$4\,1/8$	3.77	$6\,1/8$	5.60	$8\,1/8$	7.43
$1/4$	0.23	$2\,1/4$	2.06	$4\,1/4$	3.89	$6\,1/4$	5.72	$8\,1/4$	7.54
$3/8$	0.34	$2\,3/8$	2.17	$4\,3/8$	4.00	$6\,3/8$	5.83	$8\,3/8$	7.66
$1/2$	0.46	$2\,1/2$	2.29	$4\,1/2$	4.11	$6\,1/2$	5.94	$8\,1/2$	7.77
$5/8$	0.57	$2\,5/8$	2.40	$4\,5/8$	4.23	$6\,5/8$	6.06	$8\,5/8$	7.89
$3/4$	0.69	$2\,3/4$	2.51	$4\,3/4$	4.34	$6\,3/4$	6.17	$8\,3/4$	8.00
$7/8$	0.80	$2\,7/8$	2.63	$4\,7/8$	4.46	$6\,7/8$	6.29	$8\,7/8$	8.12
1	0.91	3	2.74	5	4.57	7	6.40	9	8.23
$1\,1/8$	1.03	$3\,1/8$	2.86	$5\,1/8$	4.69	$7\,1/8$	6.52	$9\,1/8$	8.34
$1\,1/4$	1.14	$3\,1/4$	2.97	$5\,1/4$	4.80	$7\,1/4$	6.63	$9\,1/4$	8.46
$1\,3/8$	1.26	$3\,3/8$	3.09	$5\,3/8$	4.91	$7\,3/8$	6.74	$9\,3/8$	8.57
$1\,1/2$	1.37	$3\,1/2$	3.20	$5\,1/2$	5.03	$7\,1/2$	6.86	$9\,1/2$	8.69
$1\,5/8$	1.49	$3\,5/8$	3.31	$5\,5/8$	5.14	$7\,5/8$	6.97	$9\,5/8$	8.80
$1\,3/4$	1.60	$3\,3/4$	3.43	$5\,3/4$	5.26	$7\,3/4$	7.09	$9\,3/4$	8.92
$1\,7/8$	1.71	$3\,7/8$	3.54	$5\,7/8$	5.37	$7\,7/8$	7.20	$9\,7/8$	9.03
2	1.83	4	3.66	6	5.49	8	7.32	10	9.14

index